ANOTHER
52 GREAT
BRIDGE TIPS

David Bird

BATSFORD

First published in the United Kingdom in 2006 by
Batsford
151 Freston Road
London
W10 6TH

An imprint of Anova Books Company Ltd

ISBN-13 9780713490480
ISBN-10 0 7134 9048 9

A CIP catalogue record for this book is available from the British Library.

10 9 8 7 6 5 4 3 2 1

Typset by Ruth Edmondson, Saltash, Devon
Printed by MPG Books Ltd, Bodmin, Cornwall

Editor: Elena Jeronimidis

This book can be ordered direct from the publisher at the website:
www.anovabooks.com, or try your local bookshop

Distributed in the United States and Canada by Sterling Publishing Co.,
387 Park Avenue South, New York, NY 10016, USA

This book is dedicated to my friend and fellow bridge writer, Tim Bourke, who has constructed hundreds of great deals for me over the years.

David Bird

CONTENTS

CONTENTS continued

Tip 1

Duck the first round when dummy holds the king

Suppose you are playing in 3NT with something like ◊A-10-8-7-3 in dummy and ◊6-4 in your hand. When entries to dummy are scarce, it is fairly obvious to duck the first round of diamonds, intending to cross to the ◊A on the second round and then duck a round of the suit.

In this Tip we look at the less well known situation where dummy's top card in the long suit is the king. It may still be good technique to duck on the first round. Look at this deal:

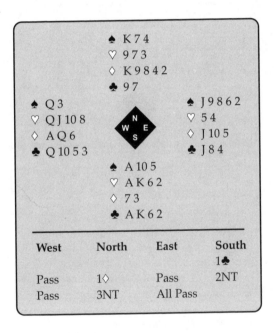

	♠ K 7 4		
	♡ 9 7 3		
	◊ K 9 8 4 2		
	♣ 9 7		

♠ Q 3   ♠ J 9 8 6 2
♡ Q J 10 8   ♡ 5 4
◊ A Q 6   ◊ J 10 5
♣ Q 10 5 3   ♣ J 8 4

♠ A 10 5
♡ A K 6 2
◊ 7 3
♣ A K 6 2

West	North	East	South
			1♣
Pass	1◊	Pass	2NT
Pass	3NT	All Pass	

How will you play 3NT when West leads the ♡Q?

It is not a good game. You have six top tricks and will need three diamond tricks to increase the total to nine. This will be possible only if West holds three diamonds to the ace. Even if this is the case, you must still play carefully. Suppose you win the first heart and play a diamond to the king. The king will win but you will score only one trick from the suit. The defenders will win the next diamond and you will have only one entry left to dummy (the ♠K), with the suit not yet established. You will go two down, despite the perfect diamond position.

To make full use of dummy's ♦K, you must duck the first round of diamonds, however strange this may seem. East wins and plays another heart. You win in your hand and play a diamond. If West rises with the ♦A, dummy's remaining ♦K-9-8 will be good. If instead he plays the ♦Q, you will cover with dummy's ♦K. Because you delayed playing the king until the second round, this entry to dummy is now useful. You can lead a third round of diamonds, setting up two long cards in the suit. The ♠K remains as an entry to reach them.

Ducking can also be a useful play when dummy's suit is headed by the king-queen:

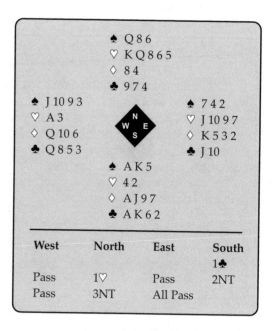

West	North	East	South
			1♣
Pass	1♡	Pass	2NT
Pass	3NT	All Pass	

How will you play 3NT when West leads the ♠J?

You have six top tricks and will need three heart tricks to carry you past the finishing line. You win the opening lead in your own hand, preserving the ♠Q as an entry to dummy. What next? Suppose you play a heart to the king. You can no longer make the contract! You return to your hand with the ♣A, let's say, to lead another heart. The ♡A goes in from West and he returns a spade. You win with the ♠Q (the last entry to dummy) and find that you have only two heart tricks. Whether you turn to clubs or diamonds, in an effort to set up a ninth trick, you will not meet with any success.

When you need only three tricks from this heart combination, you must duck the first round. East wins cheaply and returns a spade (you can cope with any other switch). You win with the ♠K and lead a second round of hearts. The ace pops up and now dummy's last three hearts are good.

It is not just against this location of the defenders' hearts that the first-round heart duck succeeds. Suppose this was the lie of the suit:

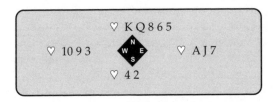

If you play to the ♡K on the first round, East will duck. You return to your hand in another suit and lead a heart to the queen. East wins with the ♡A and you will score only one heart trick. The suit is not yet established and you have only one entry (the ♠Q) left to the table. Now see what happens if you follow the Tip and duck the first round. East wins cheaply and returns a spade. You win in the South hand play a heart to the king. Whether East wins this round or the next round, you will score the three heart tricks that you need.

For our final deal we will add yet another honour to dummy's long suit, clubs on this occasion, making it ♣K-Q-J-7-3. Even then, there may be good reason to duck the first round.

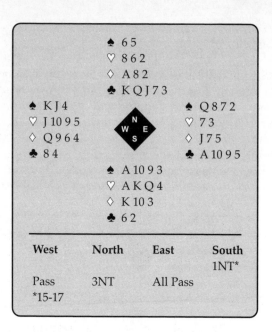

| ♠ 6 5 |
| ♡ 8 6 2 |
| ◊ A 8 2 |
| ♣ K Q J 7 3 |

♠ K J 4
♡ J 10 9 5
◊ Q 9 6 4
♣ 8 4

♠ Q 8 7 2
♡ 7 3
◊ J 7 5
♣ A 10 9 5

♠ A 10 9 3
♡ A K Q 4
◊ K 10 3
♣ 6 2

West	North	East	South
			1NT*
Pass	3NT	All Pass	
*15-17			

West leads the ♡J against 3NT and you win with the ♡A. It may seem natural to play a club to the king now but it will cost you the contract. East will hold up the ♣A. Perhaps you will return to your hand in one of the red suits for a second club lead towards dummy, in case West started with a doubleton ♣A. No such luck. East will win the second round of clubs and you will score only two club tricks, going one down.

To guard against a 4-2 division of the club suit, you must duck the first round of clubs. If East wins and switches to spades, the odds are good that your defences in this suit will suffice. When you regain the lead, you will play a club to the king, setting up the suit. The ◊A can then be used as an entry to enjoy the established winners.

It is not always right to look for a 4-4 fit

Suppose your partner opens 1NT (or 2NT) and you hold enough points for game in a hand that contains a four-card major. It is usually right to look for a 4-4 fit in the suit. Usually, yes, but not always! This Tip will describe some situations where you will fare better in the long run if you raise directly to 3NT.

The most common situation is where you have 4-3-3-3 shape. There is then a risk that there will be four losers whether you play in no-trumps or the 4-4 fit. Look at this deal:

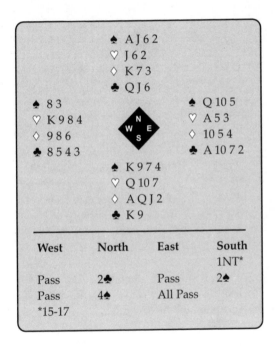

	♠ A J 6 2	
	♡ J 6 2	
	♢ K 7 3	
	♣ Q J 6	
♠ 8 3		♠ Q 10 5
♡ K 9 8 4		♡ A 5 3
♢ 9 8 6		♢ 10 5 4
♣ 8 5 4 3		♣ A 10 7 2
	♠ K 9 7 4	
	♡ Q 10 7	
	♢ A Q J 2	
	♣ K 9	

West	North	East	South
			1NT*
Pass	2♣	Pass	2♠
Pass	4♠	All Pass	
*15-17			

There were three certain losers in the side suits, so declarer needed to pick up the trumps without loss to make the spade game. It was not possible as the cards lay and he went one down.

Although bridge is not a game of certainties, it is much better tactics in the long run to raise directly to 3NT with 4-3-3-3 shape. On this deal, for example, you have six top tricks and cannot be prevented from adding three more tricks from the hearts and clubs. One deal proves nothing, you may be thinking, and you could easily change a few cards in the diagram to make 4♠ a better game. Yes, but watch any world championship (which you can do nowadays, on the internet) and you will see that the great champions always prefer 3NT when they have 4-3-3-3 shape. The odds favour this action. Give it a try and you will find out for yourself!

Even when you hold a four-card major in a hand with 4-4-3-2 shape, there may be reasons to suggest that it is not wise to look for a 4-4 fit.

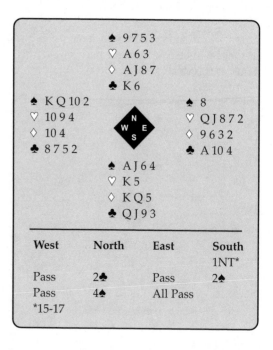

```
                    ♠ 9 7 5 3
                    ♡ A 6 3
                    ◊ A J 8 7
                    ♣ K 6
   ♠ K Q 10 2                      ♠ 8
   ♡ 10 9 4            N           ♡ Q J 8 7 2
   ◊ 10 4          W     E         ◊ 9 6 3 2
   ♣ 8 7 5 2          S            ♣ A 10 4
                    ♠ A J 6 4
                    ♡ K 5
                    ◊ K Q 5
                    ♣ Q J 9 3
```

West	North	East	South
			1NT*
Pass	2♣	Pass	2♠
Pass	4♠	All Pass	
*15-17			

The deal is from a club duplicate and the original bidding is shown. Declarer had to lose three trump tricks and the ♣A, going one down. 'What an awful trump break!' he exclaimed.

The trumps might have broken more kindly, yes, but North might also have shown more imagination in the bidding. If he responds 3NT instead, the contract will easily be made on any lead. There are seven tricks on top and two more will come from the club suit.

There were three reasons for North to raise directly to 3NT instead of seeking a 4-4 spade fit. The first was that his spades were very poor and there was a consequent risk of several losers in the suit. The second was that his doubleton holding, a potential weak spot when playing in no-trumps, was fortified by a top honour. The final reason was that he held a full 12 points. He therefore knew that the partnership had 27-29 points and there should be a good play for nine tricks in no-trumps. Had the total been only 24 or 25 points instead, there would be more reason to prefer a spade game, where ruffing tricks might be required.

It is particularly important to prefer no-trumps to a 4-4 fit when you are playing at the slam level. With 34 points between the hands, you will usually have enough strength to make 6NT. This is a typical deal:

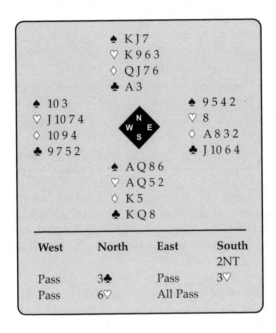

	♠ K J 7		
	♡ K 9 6 3		
	◊ Q J 7 6		
	♣ A 3		

♠ 10 3		♠ 9 5 4 2
♡ J 10 7 4		♡ 8
◊ 10 9 4		◊ A 8 3 2
♣ 9 7 5 2		♣ J 10 6 4

	♠ A Q 8 6	
	♡ A Q 5 2	
	◊ K 5	
	♣ K Q 8	

West	North	East	South
			2NT
Pass	3♣	Pass	3♡
Pass	6♡	All Pass	

Many North players would look for a 4-4 heart fit, the auction proceeding as shown in the diagram. Declarer would lose a trick in each red suit, going one down.

North holds a full 14 points opposite the 20-22 points indicated by his partner. He should appreciate that 6NT will have good play and should not risk playing in a 4-4 fit, where a bad trump break may defeat the slam. The recommended bidding is a simple 2NT – 6NT. There are ten tricks on top and two more can easily be established from the diamond suit.

Even when the potential trump suit is strong, you may prefer to play in

6NT to avoid the risk of an adverse ruff. North-South thought they were unlucky when this deal arose:

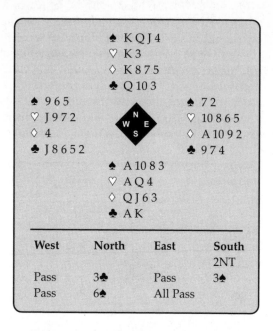

	♠ K Q J 4	
	♡ K 3	
	◇ K 8 7 5	
	♣ Q 10 3	
♠ 9 6 5		♠ 7 2
♡ J 9 7 2		♡ 10 8 6 5
◇ 4		◇ A 10 9 2
♣ J 8 6 5 2		♣ 9 7 4
	♠ A 10 8 3	
	♡ A Q 4	
	◇ Q J 6 3	
	♣ A K	

West	North	East	South
			2NT
Pass	3♣	Pass	3♠
Pass	6♠	All Pass	

West led his singleton diamond, East winning with the ace and delivering a diamond ruff. What a waste of a combined total of 34 points! Once again the bidding should have gone 2NT – 6NT. Declarer would have ten tricks on top with an easy two more available from the diamond suit.

Note that a contract of 6◇, on a 4-4 fit, would also fail. There would be two unavoidable losers in the trump suit. Balanced hands like these, containing a full 34 points, cry out to be played in no-trumps.

Tip
3

Remember the bids that were not made

Whenever one of the defenders made a bid during the auction, declarer will have valuable information at his disposal. That's obvious, yes, but it can be just as important to remember the bids that were not made! Suppose West did not open the bidding and has already shown up with 10 points. He is unlikely to hold another queen in his hand and you can confidently finesse his partner for the card. In this Tip we will look at some deals where the best play is indicated by a bid that a defender did not make.

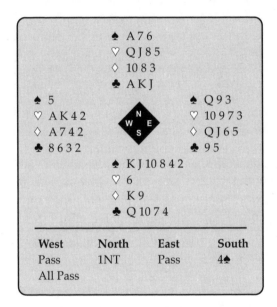

West	North	East	South
Pass	1NT	Pass	4♠
All Pass			

West leads the ♡A against your spade game and switches to the ♣6. How will you play the contract?

You can assume from the opening lead that West holds the ♡A-K. Since he is a passed hand, he will not hold both the ◊A and the ♠Q in addition. After winning the club switch with the ♣A, you should therefore cash the ♠A and then finesse the ♠J. If the finesse loses to the ♠Q with West, you can be sure that the ◊A will be onside and you will still make the contract. The finesse gains when the cards lie as in the diagram, because

---

you avoid losing a trump trick. If you play for the drop in trumps, you will go down.

On the next deal it is East's failure to respond that tells you how the cards must lie.

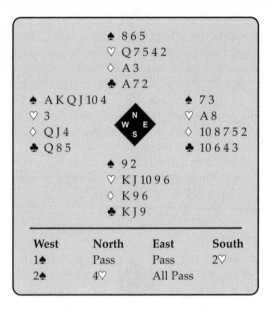

	♠ 8 6 5		
	♡ Q 7 5 4 2		
	◇ A 3		
	♣ A 7 2		

♠ A K Q J 10 4	♠ 7 3
♡ 3	♡ A 8
◇ Q J 4	◇ 10 8 7 5 2
♣ Q 8 5	♣ 10 6 4 3

	♠ 9 2		
	♡ K J 10 9 6		
	◇ K 9 6		
	♣ K J 9		

West	North	East	South
1♠	Pass	Pass	2♡
2♠	4♡	All Pass	

West leads out the three top spades and you ruff the third round. How will you continue?

If one of the defenders holds a singleton ♡A, you have the chance of an end-play. So, you cash the two top diamonds and ruff a diamond with the ♡Q. When you play a trump, East wins with the ♡A and is able to exit safely with the ♡8. What now?

It may seem that everything depends on a finesse of the ♣J. Remember, though, that East did not respond to his partner's opening bid of 1♠. He cannot therefore hold the ♣Q in addition to the ♡A that he has already shown. Your best chance is to take a backward finesse in clubs. You lead the ♣J, planning to run the card. If West decides to cover with the ♣Q, you will win with dummy's ♣A and finesse the ♣9 on the second round.

On the final deal for this Tip it is West's failure to overcall that gives you a vital clue to the lie of the cards.

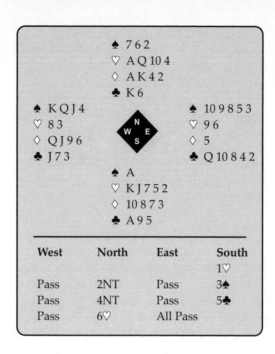

	♠ 7 6 2		
	♡ A Q 10 4		
	◊ A K 4 2		
	♣ K 6		

♠ K Q J 4		♠ 10 9 8 5 3
♡ 8 3		♡ 9 6
◊ Q J 9 6		◊ 5
♣ J 7 3		♣ Q 10 8 4 2

	♠ A		
	♡ K J 7 5 2		
	◊ 10 8 7 3		
	♣ A 9 5		

West	North	East	South
			1♡
Pass	2NT	Pass	3♠
Pass	4NT	Pass	5♣
Pass	6♡	All Pass	

North shows a strong heart raise with a Jacoby 2NT response and South's 3♠ rebid indicates a singleton spade. How will you play the slam when West leads the ♠K?

The only risk is a 4-1 (or 5-0) diamond break and an elimination play will assist you in overcoming this. You win the spade lead and draw trumps in two rounds. You then ruff two spades in your hand and one club in the dummy, eliminating the black suits. West drops the jack on the third round of spades; he also drops the jack on the third round of clubs. If these cards are to be believed, his shape will be 4-2-4-3 or 4-2-3-4. In other words, if anyone holds four diamonds, it will be him.

Defenders do sometimes drop false cards, hoping to mislead the declarer about the distribution. Here, however, you have back-up evidence from the auction. West began with two hearts. If he holds a singleton diamond, his hand would be something like ♠K-Q-J-10-4 ♡8-3 ◊6 ♣Q-J-7-4-3. He would then surely have overcalled 1♠ or bid a Michaels 2♡. You should therefore conclude that it is West, if anyone, who will hold four diamonds. On that assumption, what is the best play in diamonds? These cards remain:

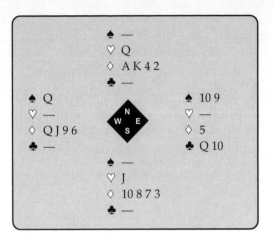

You should lead the ◊8, planning to run the card. If East wins with a singleton 9, jack or queen, he will have to concede a ruff-and-discard with his return. If he wins and is able to return a diamond, the suit will break 3-2. It will do West no good to cover the ◊8 with the ◊9 (or a deceptive ◊J or ◊Q). You will win with dummy's ◊A and continue with a low diamond to the ten. West will have to win the trick and lead away from his remaining diamond honour, or give a ruff-and-discard.

Suppose that the clues from the bidding, and the fall of the cards, had led you to believe that it would be East, if anyone, who held four diamonds. How would you play the suit then? You would cash the ◊A and lead low towards the ◊10 on the second round. If East rose with the queen or jack from ◊Q-J-x-x, he would have to lead into the split K-10 tenace on his return (or give you a ruff-and-discard).

Tip
4

Cash your
winners before
a trump promotion

Promoting an extra trump trick in defence is one of the most satisfying plays that the game offers. Sometimes declarer can dodge the blow by discarding a loser as you attempt the trump promotion. To avoid this, you may need to cash one or more side-suit winners before leading the card that partner can ruff. Look at this deal:

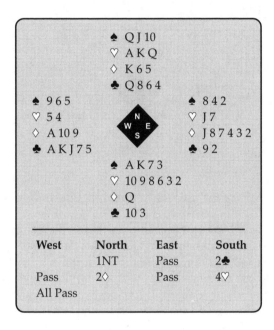

	♠ Q J 10	
	♡ A K Q	
	◇ K 6 5	
	♣ Q 8 6 4	
♠ 9 6 5		♠ 8 4 2
♡ 5 4		♡ J 7
◇ A 10 9		◇ J 8 7 4 3 2
♣ A K J 7 5		♣ 9 2
	♠ A K 7 3	
	♡ 10 9 8 6 3 2	
	◇ Q	
	♣ 10 3	

West	North	East	South
	1NT	Pass	2♣
Pass	2◇	Pass	4♡
All Pass			

Sitting West, you lead the ♣K and see East signal with the ♣9. You continue with the ♣A and both the closed hands follow suit. How can the contract be beaten?

South's sequence suggests that he holds six hearts. Since he began with a Stayman response, he must also hold four spades. You know he began with two clubs, so his shape is almost certainly 4-6-1-2. There is no point leading the ◇10 at trick three, hoping that South holds ◇J-x and will guess wrongly. South has only one diamond! What else can you try?

A third round of clubs will promote East's ♡J, should he hold that card.

What will happen if you lead a third round of clubs straight away, though? East will ruff triumphantly with the ♡J, yes, but declarer will counter by discarding his singleton diamond. The contract will be made.

To prevent declarer from rescuing his contract in this fashion, you must cash the ◇A at trick three. The way will then be clear for you to lead a third round of clubs, promoting East's ♡J into the setting trick.

Let's change that deal, giving East the ◇A. The winning defence would then be considerably more difficult.

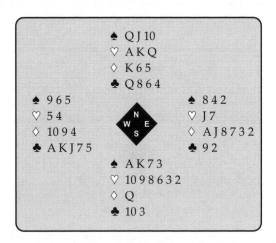

Again you lead the ♣K, East playing the ♣9. Two more clubs will give the defenders three tricks, provided East holds the ♡J. You need a fourth trick, though, and this can only be the ◇A or the ♠A. Declarer is more likely to hold the ♠A since he has four spades and only one diamond. Since the ◇A needs to be scored before declarer has a chance to discard his singleton, West should switch to a diamond at trick two!

East wins with the ◇A, the ◇Q falling from South, and switches back to clubs. West wins with the ♣A and leads a third round of clubs to promote a trump trick for East. Not easy, I'm sure you agree, but that is how you need to defend to beat the contract.

Move to the East seat now, as we see one more deal on this theme:

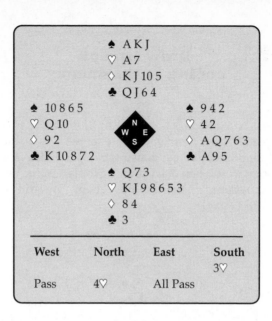

West leads the ◊9, covered by the ◊10 in dummy, and you win with the ◊Q. How should you continue the defence?

It is not good practice to lead a nine from 9-x-x. (In Europe it is popular to lead the middle card; in the USA many players lead the bottom card.) So, West holds either one diamond or two. You continue with the ◊A and both the closed hands follow suit. What next?

A third round of diamonds will promote a trump trick if West holds the ♡K or ♡Q-10. Suppose you play a third diamond immediately, though. South will discard his singleton club. West can ruff with the ♡10 but this will be the last trick for the defence. The contract will be made. Instead you should cash the ♣A. West can see that a third round of diamonds will promote a trump trick for him. He will therefore discourage a club continuation by signalling with the ♣2. You switch back to diamonds and declarer is doomed, whichever trump he plays on this trick.

There is a second reason why you should cash the ♣A at trick three. Suppose West's trumps were something like ♡6-5 and there was no hope of a trump promotion. Holding the ♣K he would signal with a high club to suggest a club continuation. You would still deliver a diamond ruff when South held three diamonds, of course. When South held only two diamonds, you would play a second round of clubs instead, beating the contract if South held two cards in the suit.

Draw trumps ending in the dummy

A frequently used technique is to establish a side suit in dummy and then to reach it by 'drawing trumps, ending in the dummy.' In other words, you delay drawing the last trump until you have established a winner or two in the dummy. We will start with a straightforward example:

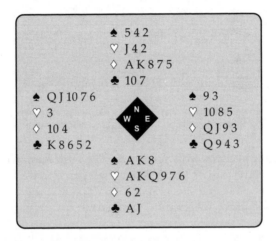

```
                 ♠ 5 4 2
                 ♡ J 4 2
                 ◇ A K 8 7 5
                 ♣ 10 7
 ♠ Q J 10 7 6              ♠ 9 3
 ♡ 3            N          ♡ 10 8 5
 ◇ 10 4      W     E       ◇ Q J 9 3
 ♣ K 8 6 5 2    S          ♣ Q 9 4 3
                 ♠ A K 8
                 ♡ A K Q 9 7 6
                 ◇ 6 2
                 ♣ A J
```

A club lead would have worked well, as it happens, but West leads the obvious ♠Q against your contract of 6♡. How will you play?

You have two potential black-suit losers and will need to set up at least one long card in diamonds, to give you a discard. You win the spade lead and draw one round of trumps with the ace. What next?

In order to make the slam when diamonds break 4-2, your next move must be to duck a diamond. Let's say that East wins and returns a club. You rise with the ♣A and draw a second round of trumps with the king, West showing out. You cannot draw the last trump at this stage. You must aim to establish the diamonds and then 'draw trumps, ending in the dummy.'

You play a diamond to the ace and everyone follows. Excellent! You ruff a diamond with the ♡Q, West showing out, and return to dummy with the ♡J. You can then cash two diamond winners, the king and the eight, discarding your two black-suit losers.

Suppose you had drawn a second round of trumps, with the king, before turning your attention to diamonds. Not good enough! When you ducked a round of diamonds, East could then return a trump, killing the trump entry to dummy before you were ready to use it.

On the next deal the defenders threaten to shorten dummy's trumps, which will prevent you from 'drawing trumps, ending in the dummy'. How can you counter this defence?

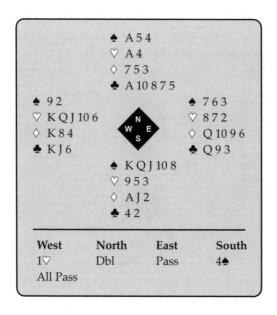

West	North	East	South
1♡	Dbl	Pass	4♠
All Pass			

How will you play the spade game when West leads the ♡K?

You win immediately, since a diamond switch would be unwelcome. You can count five trump tricks and three aces – a total of eight. One heart ruff in dummy would not help much because you would still need to set up the clubs. Your best chance is to play for a 3-3 club break.

Play one round of trumps, to the king, and then duck a round of clubs. (You duck because you want to use the ♣A as an entry on the next round.) Let's say that East wins the first round of clubs and the defenders play two more rounds of hearts. What then?

If you ruff the third round of hearts you will go down. You hope to establish the clubs with one ruff and will then need to 'draw trumps, ending in the dummy'. You cannot do this if you have taken a ruff there. So, discard a diamond from dummy on the third round of hearts. You win the defenders' switch, draw a second round of trumps with the king and cross to the ♣A. A club ruff establishes the suit, you are pleased to see, and you cross to the ace of trumps. You can then discard two diamonds on the good clubs. The game is yours.

What if East switches to the ◊10 after winning the first club? You would have to rise with the ◊A. If instead you let the defenders score a diamond trick, two more rounds of hearts would defeat you. You would have to ruff the third heart and could not then enjoy the long clubs.

We will end with a deal that is slightly different. You give up a trump trick that you might not need to concede, to guarantee that you can 'draw trumps, ending in the dummy'.

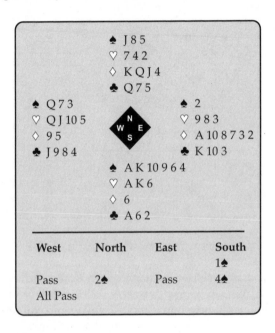

West	North	East	South
			1♠
Pass	2♠	Pass	4♠
All Pass			

How will you play the spade game when West leads the ♡Q?

You win with the ♡A and draw one round of trumps with the ♠A, everyone following. Your next move is to lead the ◊6 and West plays the ◊9, to signal his doubleton. The ◊K is played from dummy and East wins with the ◊A. You win the heart continuation with the king and must consider your next move carefully. What is it to be?

If you play the ♠K next, all will be well if the ♠Q falls. Not only will you escape a loser in trumps, dummy's ♠J will act as an entry to the ◊Q-J. You will be able to throw two losers, ending with an overtrick. When trumps are 3-1, however, the situation will not be so good. You will have four losers even when the ♣K is onside.

A better idea is to lead a low trump towards dummy's ♠J-8 at trick five. What can West do? If he rises with the ♠Q, you can win his return and cross to the ♠J (drawing trumps, ending in the dummy) to enjoy the two diamond winners. If instead West plays low, you will reach dummy immediately with the ♠8. You can then play the ◊Q, discarding one loser, intending to continue with the ◊J and discard another loser. Even if West began with a singleton diamond and can ruff the ◊Q, you will still make the contract. You would win his return, cross to the ♠J and discard another loser on the ◊J.

Tip 6

Treat a fourth-suit bid as forcing to game

When the bidding starts with non-jump bids in three different suits (for example 1◊ – 1♠ – 2♣) it is common practice among good players to treat a bid in the fourth suit, 2♡ here, as conventional. It shows a strong hand but does not promise a heart suit, or anything whatsoever in hearts. Indeed, if you did hold good heart values, you would usually be able to bid some number of no-trumps at your second turn.

That idea is generally accepted worldwide and there are many bidding situations where it is hard to understand how players survived without 'fourth suit forcing' in the early days of the game. The modern trend, however, is to play a fourth-suit bid as not only forcing but forcing to game and that is the recommendation in this Tip.

Suppose the bidding started in this fashion and you are sitting West.

(1)	(2)	(3)
♠ 4	♠ 9 4	♠ Q 2
♡ J 6	♡ K 7	♡ 8 3
◊ A K 9 7 3	◊ K Q J 6 2	◊ A Q J 8 4
♣ A Q J 8 2	♣ A J 5 4	♣ A K 7 2

West	East
1◊	1♠
2♣	2♡
?	

Let's suppose first that you are using the original method, where 2♡ shows around 11 points or more but is not forcing to game. What should you bid on the first hand? You would like to rebid your clubs. If 3♣ is not forcing, you would have to bid 4♣ instead. This is not satisfactory, since it will carry you past 3NT. It is much better to play 2♡ forcing to game, allowing you to rebid 3♣.

It's the same with (2). Holding a heart stopper, you want to bid no-

Another 52 Great Bridge Tips

trumps next. If 2NT is non-forcing, you will have to waste space by leaping to 3NT – not at all desirable with only one heart stopper. If your system allows you to bid 2NT (forcing), your partner will have the space to show a club or diamond fit. He can also to rebid his spades. You will have much more space to investigate alternative denominations.

On hand (3) you can bid a convenient 2♣, provided the auction is forcing to game. If that would be non-forcing, you will have to make some less descriptive bid at the three-level – either 3♡ or 3♠.

So, the recommendation is to play a fourth-suit bid as forcing to game and to seek a limit bid when you have around 11 points. You must give up bidding the fourth suit when you hold an 'awkward 11-count'. What does that expression mean? It means that you have no fit for partner, no good suit of your own and no stopper in the unbid suit. You therefore have no convenient limit bid. What can you bid on such hands when a bid in the fourth suit would force you to game? You mentally subtract a couple of points and make the appropriate sign-off. In other words, you underbid – justifiably when you have no fit and no stopper in the unbid suit.

Suppose the bidding starts like this and you are sitting East.

	(4)		(5)		(6)
♠	K Q 8 5 2	♠	A K J 9 4	♠	K 10 9 8 2
♡	J 6	♡	7	♡	J
◇	9 7 3	◇	9 8 6 2	◇	8 5 4 3
♣	A J 4	♣	K 5 4	♣	A K 7

West	East
1♡	1♠
2♣	?

On (4) you are not strong enough to force to game with 2◇. Mentally subtract the ♠Q and rebid 2♡, the sign-off you would make if you held a 9-count. If partner passes, he will usually be glad to have stopped so low. On (5) you would rebid 2♠ and on (6) you would raise to 3♣.

You may consider that you are losing out slightly on the 'awkward 11-counts'. Remember how much you are gaining, though, on all the stronger hands – a considerable amount of bidding space. Remember also that most top players are already following this Tip!

Tip 7

A jack lead is rarely from K-J-10

What is your reaction when a jack is led against a suit contract? Such a lead is rarely made from a holding headed by the K-J-10. You should therefore place a missing king of the suit with your right-hand opponent. Let's see a couple of deals where you can put this Tip to good use.

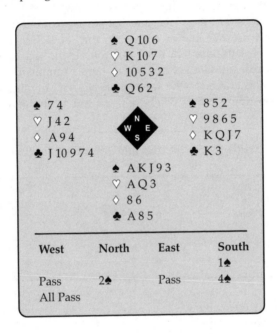

```
                    ♠ Q 10 6
                    ♡ K 10 7
                    ◊ 10 5 3 2
                    ♣ Q 6 2
   ♠ 7 4                         ♠ 8 5 2
   ♡ J 4 2          N            ♡ 9 8 6 5
   ◊ A 9 4       W     E         ◊ K Q J 7
   ♣ J 10 9 7 4     S            ♣ K 3
                    ♠ A K J 9 3
                    ♡ A Q 3
                    ◊ 8 6
                    ♣ A 8 5
```

West	North	East	South
			1♠
Pass	2♠	Pass	4♠
All Pass			

West leads the ♣J against 4♠. How will you play the contract?

You sometimes see declarers calling for dummy's ♣Q on this sort of deal. It is a poor idea. Apart from the fact that East may hold a singleton ♣K, there is nothing to be gained from the play. In the unlikely event that West has led from the ♣K-J-10, you can lead towards the ♣Q later.

You win the club lead with the ace and draw trumps in three rounds. You can mark time by exiting in diamonds but eventually you will have to tackle clubs yourself. Should you play a club to the queen or duck the second round, hoping that East began with ♣K-x? It is better to duck.

Players rarely lead from K-J-10-x but they are more than happy to lead from J-10-9-x-x. The fact that West has chosen to lead the suit should sway you towards playing East for ♣K-x. You should do the same if West wins one of the diamond tricks and continues with the ♣10.

The situation is even more clear-cut on this deal:

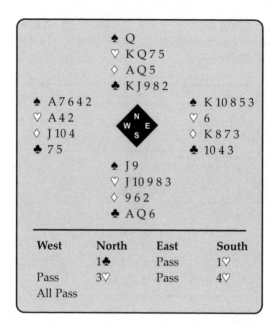

West leads the ◊J against 4♡. How will you play the contract?

If the lead is from ◊K-J-10, you can finesse the ◊Q and knock out the ♡A. You will then be able to draw trumps and discard your remaining diamond loser on dummy's clubs, scoring an overtrick. Even in a Pairs event, where overtricks are heavily rewarded, this would not be the right line of play. East would win with the ◊K and clear the diamonds. You would then lose two diamonds and two aces, going one down.

A better idea is to rise with the ◊A at trick one. This will leave the diamond suit 'frozen'. What does that mean? It means that neither defender can safely play the suit again. (If West leads the ◊4, you will play low from dummy, forcing East's ◊K.) You lead the ♡K, which West wins, and the defenders can score only two more tricks. When you regain the lead, you will draw trumps and run the clubs, claiming the contract.

Hold up an ace to prevent declarer finessing

In this Tip we will see how you should hold up an ace, or some other high card, to stop declarer reaching dummy to take a finesse. You are sitting East on this deal:

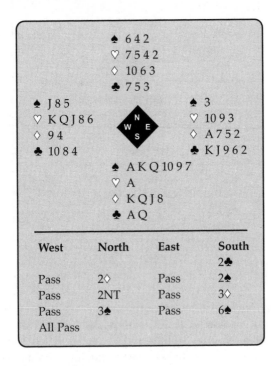

		♠ 6 4 2	
		♡ 7 5 4 2	
		♢ 10 6 3	
		♣ 7 5 3	
♠ J 8 5			♠ 3
♡ K Q J 8 6			♡ 10 9 3
♢ 9 4			♢ A 7 5 2
♣ 10 8 4			♣ K J 9 6 2
		♠ A K Q 10 9 7	
		♡ A	
		♢ K Q J 8	
		♣ A Q	

West	North	East	South
			2♣
Pass	2♢	Pass	2♠
Pass	2NT	Pass	3♢
Pass	3♠	Pass	6♠
All Pass			

Declarer wins the ♡K lead and draws trumps in three rounds. His next move is to lead the ♢K from his hand, West following with the ♢9. What is your plan for the defence?

South would not have bid a slam with two likely losers in his hand, so he surely began with a singleton ♡A. To justify his bidding, he must also hold all the missing honours in the minor suits. Suppose you win the ♢K with the ♢A. He will ruff your heart return, cross to the ♢10 and finesse the ♣Q successfully. To beat the contract, you must keep declarer out of the dummy, preventing him from leading towards his club tenace. You allow the ♢K to win and South continues with the ♢Q, West completing a high-low. Placing South with four diamonds, you duck again. When declarer plays a third diamond to dummy's ten, you win with the ace and return a heart. Declarer cannot reach the dummy and eventually has to concede a trick to your ♣K. One down!

Sometimes you must hold up an ace at trick one. Stay in the East seat for this deal:

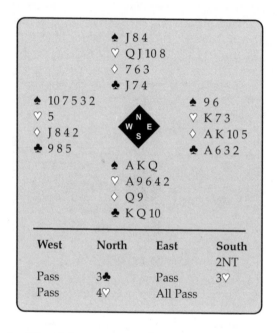

West	North	East	South
			2NT
Pass	3♣	Pass	3♡
Pass	4♡	All Pass	

West leads the ♣9 and dummy plays the ♣4. How will you defend?

If you win with the ♣A, declarer will unblock one of his top honours. He will then be able to cross to the ♣J to take a trump finesse. Instead, you should play low on the first trick, South winning with the ♣K. Suppose he leads the ◊Q next. You must cash two rounds of diamonds and exit with a spade. If declarer leads the ♣Q next, you will duck again. You can then win a third round of clubs and exit safely with a third round of diamonds, preventing declarer from reaching the dummy. The ♡K will be the setting trick.

Tip

9

Test the side suit while there is still a trump out

We are taught in our cradles to draw trumps straight away. Sometimes players find themselves sitting back in their chairs, half way through the hand, wishing that there was still a trump left in the dummy. Declarer played carelessly on this deal:

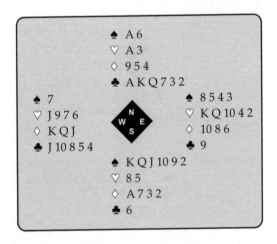

```
              ♠ A 6
              ♡ A 3
              ◇ 9 5 4
              ♣ A K Q 7 3 2
  ♠ 7                        ♠ 8 5 4 3
  ♡ J 9 7 6        N         ♡ K Q 10 4 2
  ◇ K Q J      W     E       ◇ 10 8 6
  ♣ J 10 8 5 4     S         ♣ 9
              ♠ K Q J 10 9 2
              ♡ 8 5
              ◇ A 7 3 2
              ♣ 6
```

South ended in 6♠ and West led the ◇K. How would you tackle the deal?

Declarer won with the ◇A, drew trumps in four rounds and turned to the club suit. If it had broken 4-2, all would have been well. Declarer could have established the suit with one ruff and returned to dummy with the ♡A. As it was, the 5-1 club break defeated the contract.

Drawing trumps straight away is a mistake because you will need the ♠A entry to set up the clubs if they happen to break 5-1. After winning the diamond lead, you should cross to the ♣A and ruff a club high. If both defenders follow to two rounds of clubs, you can draw trumps and cross to the ♡A to enjoy the established clubs. When the cards lie as in the diagram, East will show out on the second club. You ruff in your hand, cross to the ♠A and ruff another club. Only then do you draw trumps before returning to dummy with the ♡A to discard three red-suit losers on the ♣K-Q-7.

Another 52 Great Bridge Tips

On the next deal, from an international match between New Zealand and Chinese Taipei, dummy's third trump may be needed for a ruff.

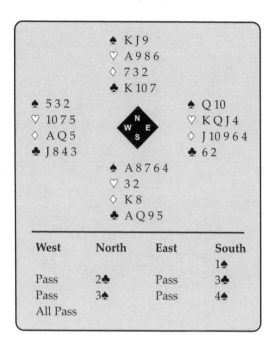

		♠ K J 9	
		♡ A 9 8 6	
		◊ 7 3 2	
		♣ K 10 7	
♠ 5 3 2			♠ Q 10
♡ 10 7 5			♡ K Q J 4
◊ A Q 5			◊ J 10 9 6 4
♣ J 8 4 3			♣ 6 2
		♠ A 8 7 6 4	
		♡ 3 2	
		◊ K 8	
		♣ A Q 9 5	

West	North	East	South
			1♠
Pass	2♣	Pass	3♣
Pass	3♠	Pass	4♠
All Pass			

West led a trump, which somewhat unluckily gave away the position in that suit. Declarer won East's ten with the ace and, since West would not have led from the queen, continued with a trump to dummy's king. The queen duly appeared from East. How should you continue the play?

The original declarer drew the last trump and led a diamond to the king. This lost to the ace and declarer subsequently lost a club trick to go one down. Can you see a better line of play?

Before drawing the last trump, you should test the club suit. Both defenders follow to the ace and king. When a third round is led from dummy, East shows out but has no trump left. You win with the club queen and ruff your last club with dummy's last trump. You lose just three tricks in the red suits, making the game exactly.

Nothing is lost by playing in the recommended fashion. If clubs break 3-3, or the ♣J falls in two rounds, you will simply draw the last trump. What if clubs are 4-2 and West ruffs your third club honour? You can ruff the fourth round of clubs with dummy's last trump and will still make the contract when the ◊A is onside.

Next we will see a deal where you test the side suit before drawing the last trump because you may need to take a finesse there:

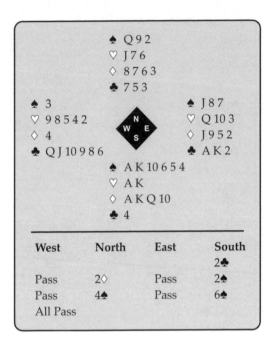

	♠ Q 9 2		
	♡ J 7 6		
	◊ 8 7 6 3		
	♣ 7 5 3		

West leads the ♣Q, somewhat surprised to win the first trick, and continues with another club. How will you play the contract?

You ruff the second club and cash the ♠A-K, West showing out on the second round. Suppose you draw the last trump straight away. You will be in dummy for the last time, with no idea whether you need to take a diamond finesse. A better idea is to test the diamonds before drawing the last trump. When you play the ace and king of diamonds, West shows out on the second round. Delighted at this turn of events, you cross to dummy with the ♠Q. You can then finesse the ◊10 and claim the contract.

Nothing can be done when West holds ◊J-x-x-x. It's true that by playing in the recommended fashion you will go two down, instead of one down. Still, that is a tiny premium to pay for the extra chance of making the slam.

The final deal for this Tip is slightly more difficult but follows the same theme. Take the South cards here:

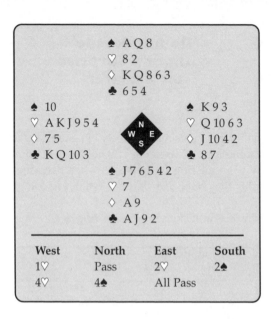

	♠ A Q 8	
	♡ 8 2	
	◊ K Q 8 6 3	
	♣ 6 5 4	
♠ 10		♠ K 9 3
♡ A K J 9 5 4		♡ Q 10 6 3
◊ 7 5		◊ J 10 4 2
♣ K Q 10 3		♣ 8 7
	♠ J 7 6 5 4 2	
	♡ 7	
	◊ A 9	
	♣ A J 9 2	

West	North	East	South
1♡	Pass	2♡	2♠
4♡	4♠	All Pass	

West leads the ♡K against your spade game and continues with the ♡A. You ruff the second heart and play a trump to the queen, losing to the king. Back comes the ♣8. How will you play from this point?

You win with the ♣A and cash the ♠J, West discarding a heart. If you draw East's last trump immediately, you will need the diamonds to break 3-3. A better idea is to play the ◊A-K and to lead a third round of the suit. If diamonds do indeed break 3-3, only an overtrick has been lost. You will ruff in the South hand and re-enter dummy with the ♠A to enjoy the rest of the diamond suit. The benefit of this line is displayed when East holds four diamonds. You ruff the third round of diamonds in your hand and West cannot overruff because he has no trumps left. The diamond suit is established and you cross to the ♠A, claiming ten tricks and the contract.

Tip
10

Do not double
without a surprise
for declarer

When the opponents reach a freely bid game or slam, you should not double merely because you hold a lot of points. They knew they were missing those points when they decided to bid so high. Presumably they have distributional values to compensate.

West thought he was unlucky on the following deal:

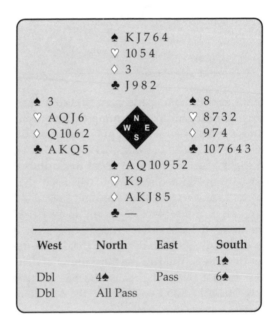

	♠ K J 7 6 4		
	♡ 10 5 4		
	◇ 3		
	♣ J 9 8 2		

♠ 3		♠ 8
♡ A Q J 6		♡ 8 7 3 2
◇ Q 10 6 2		◇ 9 7 4
♣ A K Q 5		♣ 10 7 6 4 3

	♠ A Q 10 9 5 2	
	♡ K 9	
	◇ A K J 8 5	
	♣ —	

West	North	East	South
			1♠
Dbl	4♠	Pass	6♠
Dbl	All Pass		

West could not believe that a slam had been bid. He doubled and led the ♣A. When this was ruffed, West shook his head as if it was very bad luck. Declarer drew trumps and set up the diamonds with two ruffs. Two of dummy's hearts were then discarded and the slam was made.

'Can you believe it?' West exclaimed. 'I had 18 points!'

West's double of the slam was unwise. South had not bid Blackwood, so it was likely that he would be void in one suit, probably clubs. He had not been forced to bid a slam, so presumably he felt he had a good chance of making twelve tricks. West had no 'surprise' for declarer in his hand. South knew that his partner's raise to 4♠ was pre-emptive and had contracted for twelve tricks despite missing West's 18 points.

The main reason not to double is that there is no need to. Suppose South has overbid and goes one down. You will get a good board anyway! At the other table (or tables, if it is a Pairs) the contract is unlikely to be a slam and you will fare excellently for one down undoubled.

Suppose next that the opponents bid 1♠ – 4♠ – 6♠ and you hold this hand over the opening bidder:

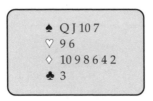

```
♠ Q J 10 7
♡ 9 6
♢ 10 9 8 6 4 2
♣ 3
```

Only three points, but the hand is a better double of 6♠ than the 18-count because you have a nasty surprise for declarer. You are almost certain to score two trump tricks. On some deals, you would still not double in case the opponents ran to 6NT and could make that. On this auction, it is almost inconceivable that 6NT can be made. Perhaps this is the lay-out:

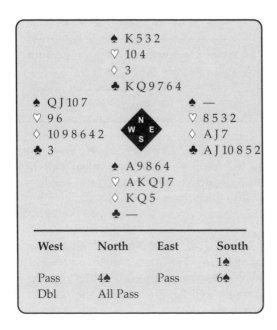

```
          ♠ K 5 3 2
          ♡ 10 4
          ♢ 3
          ♣ K Q 9 7 6 4
♠ Q J 10 7              ♠ —
♡ 9 6                   ♡ 8 5 3 2
♢ 10 9 8 6 4 2         ♢ A J 7
♣ 3                    ♣ A J 10 8 5 2
          ♠ A 9 8 6 4
          ♡ A K Q J 7
          ♢ K Q 5
          ♣ —
```

West	North	East	South
			1♠
Pass	4♠	Pass	6♠
Dbl	All Pass		

You lead the ◇10 and the contract goes two down. 'I couldn't believe it when you doubled,' your partner says, after the contract has gone two down. 'I held two aces!'

As you see, the slam did not go down because declarer was missing 13 points. It went down because the trumps did not break 2-2.

Another type of double that you see all too frequently is a double of 3NT made because one defender holds 10 points or so and his partner has overcalled. When the opponents bid 3NT they will generally hold at least 24 points between them, probably more. If you have a fair hand and partner has overcalled, you should conclude that he has very few points.

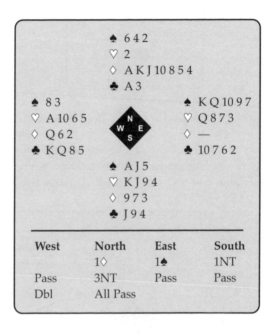

	♠ 6 4 2		
	♡ 2		
	◇ A K J 10 8 5 4		
	♣ A 3		

♠ 8 3   ♠ K Q 10 9 7
♡ A 10 6 5   ♡ Q 8 7 3
◇ Q 6 2   ◇ —
♣ K Q 8 5   ♣ 10 7 6 2

	♠ A J 5		
	♡ K J 9 4		
	◇ 9 7 3		
	♣ J 9 4		

West	North	East	South
	1◇	1♠	1NT
Pass	3NT	Pass	Pass
Dbl	All Pass		

West led the ♠8 and declarer allowed East's ♠Q to win the first trick. East switched to the ♡Q, hoping to take two or three tricks in that suit (there could hardly be four tricks available or declarer would not have ducked the first trick). The queen was covered by the king and ace and West returned another heart, declarer winning with the ♡9.

A diamond to the ace revealed the 3-0 break and declarer returned to his hand by finessing the ♠J. The marked diamond finesse brought in that suit and declarer scored two doubled overtricks, giving him a score of +1150. North might well have redoubled the contract and the score would then have been +1800.

'I had 11 points, partner!' exclaimed West, 'I had to double after you had overcalled.'

Have you ever heard anything so foolish? It was clear that North would hold a long diamond suit over him and the ◊Q would be worth nothing in defence. Also, South's spade honours would be well placed, sitting over East. There was no reason whatsoever to double. If North had overbid and the contract went down, it would be a good result for East-West anyway. Putting it another way, West had no surprise for the opponents.

East had a much better double of 3NT on this deal:

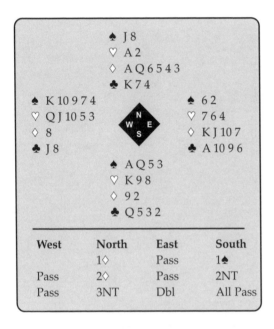

West	North	East	South
	1◊	Pass	1♠
Pass	2◊	Pass	2NT
Pass	3NT	Dbl	All Pass

Sitting East, what are your thoughts when North bids 3NT? The opponents' values are limited, because North rebid only 2◊ and South showed around 11 points with his 2NT. You know also that the diamond suit lies badly for declarer and will be difficult to establish. Partner may well have something good in spades, stacked over South's bid suit.

It may not be a 100% certainty but the prospects are good for a penalty double. As the cards lie, the game will go two down, whether West leads the ♡Q or the ◊8. Look out for such doubles when the cards lie poorly for declarer and the opponents have limited their hands.

Tip
11

Compare the win-lose holdings

Y ou can often choose between two lines of play by counting the defensive holdings against which they will succeed. If one line will win against four holdings and the other will win against six, choose the second line. How do you perform the calculation? Let's see an example.

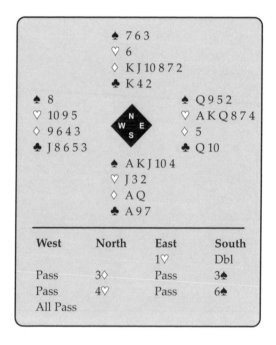

```
                    ♠ 7 6 3
                    ♡ 6
                    ◇ K J 10 8 7 2
                    ♣ K 4 2
    ♠ 8                          ♠ Q 9 5 2
    ♡ 10 9 5          N          ♡ A K Q 8 7 4
    ◇ 9 6 4 3      W     E       ◇ 5
    ♣ J 8 6 5 3       S          ♣ Q 10
                    ♠ A K J 10 4
                    ♡ J 3 2
                    ◇ A Q
                    ♣ A 9 7
```

West	North	East	South
		1♡	Dbl
Pass	3◇	Pass	3♠
Pass	4♡	Pass	6♠
All Pass			

An ambitious auction carries you to 6♠ and West leads the ♡10, East winning with the ♡Q. He continues with the ♡A, forcing dummy to ruff. How will you play the slam?

If you can pick up the trump suit without loss the contract is yours. You have only two trumps left in the dummy. Should you finesse the ♠J on the first round? Or should you cash the ♠A, to catch a singleton ♠Q offside, intending to return to the ♣K to finesse on the second round of trumps?

You often see players cashing the ace first in these situations. ('It was a safety play against a singleton queen offside,' they say.) Cashing the ace gains against only one holding with West, a singleton queen. If instead West began with a singleton ♣9, ♣8, ♣5 or ♣2, you do better to take two finesses. So, it is four times as good to finesse on the first round.

You get the idea, then. You count the 'win' and 'lose' defensive holdings and simply compare the two numbers. Try this slightly harder deal:

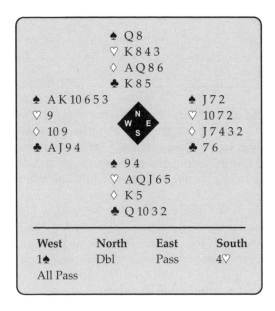

West	North	East	South
1♠	Dbl	Pass	4♡
All Pass			

West leads the ♠K and East plays the ♠2 to indicate an odd number of cards in the suit. West cashes the ♠A and switches to the ◇10. How will you play the contract?

You win with the ◇K and draw trumps in three rounds, noting that West started with a singleton in the suit. You then play two more diamond winners and ruff dummy's last diamond, West showing out on the third round. You now have a complete count on West's hand. He began with 6-1-2-4 shape and you have reached this end position:

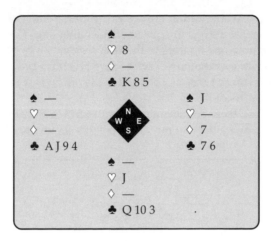

The opening bid marks West with the ♣A but who has the ♣J? If East has it, you must play a club to the king and a club back. If instead West holds ♣A-J-x-x, you can win by leading the ♣Q. When West wins with the ace, he will have to lead away from the ♣J (or give a ruff-and-discard if he has kept three clubs and a spade). What line should you follow?

East might hold these low doubletons: 9-7, 9-6, 9-4, 7-6, 7-4 or 6-4. That is six possibilities. How many jack doubleton holdings are there? J-9, J-7, J-6 or J-4. Only four. So the odds are 6-to-4 in favour of playing West for the jack. You lead the ♣Q and do indeed make the contract.

What do you make of this spade situation:

You lead a low card to the ♠J on the first round, losing to the ♠Q. When you subsequently lead a low spade towards dummy on the second round, West produces the ♠8. Should you finesse or play for the drop?

If you are not familiar with the situation, you may be surprised to hear that the odds are roughly 2-to-1 in favour of the finesse at this stage. It is an example of the Principle of Restricted Choice. You should assume that East won with the ♠Q on the first round because he had to, rather than because he chose the card from ♠K-Q doubleton.

Whether or not you understand (or accept) the idea of Restricted Choice, you can arrive at the right answer by counting the 'win' and 'lose' holdings. If you take two finesses whenever the first finesse loses and West follows low on the second round, you will win in two cases – when East holds a singleton ♠Q or a singleton ♠K. You will lose in only one case, when East holds ♠K-Q doubleton. So, that explains the 2-to-1 odds in your favour. Here is a whole deal featuring Restricted Choice:

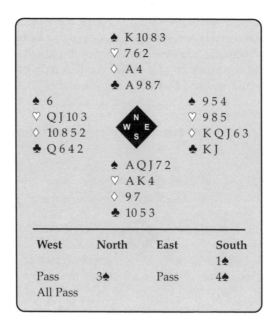

	♠ K 10 8 3		
	♡ 7 6 2		
	◊ A 4		
	♣ A 9 8 7		

♠ 6		♠ 9 5 4
♡ Q J 10 3		♡ 9 8 5
◊ 10 8 5 2		◊ K Q J 6 3
♣ Q 6 4 2		♣ K J

	♠ A Q J 7 2	
	♡ A K 4	
	◊ 9 7	
	♣ 10 5 3	

West	North	East	South
			1♠
Pass	3♠	Pass	4♠
All Pass			

You win the ♡Q lead and draw trumps. You now need a second club trick, so you can throw a red-suit loser. You lead to the ♣7, losing to the ♣J and East returns the ◊K. You win in dummy, cross to a trump and run the ♣10 to East's ♣K. East cashes a diamond and knocks out the ♡K. You lead the ♣5 towards dummy's ♣A-8 and West produces the last outstanding spot card. It is decision time. Should you finesse or not?

Yes, you should! Following such a line (after two losing finesses and a low club appearing from West on the third round) will win against ♣K-Q, ♣K-J and ♣Q-J. It will lose only to ♣K-Q-J. So, the odds are 3-to-1 in favour of a third-round finesse in clubs.

Tip 12

Rise with an honour to kill dummy's suit

When declarer has a long suit in a dummy that contains no side entries, it will often suit him to duck the first round. By doing so, he will retain dummy's honours, so that he can cross on the second round and then enjoy the remainder of the suit. As a defender in the second seat, you may be able to thwart declarer's plan by playing high in the second seat and that is the subject of this Tip. Take the West cards here:

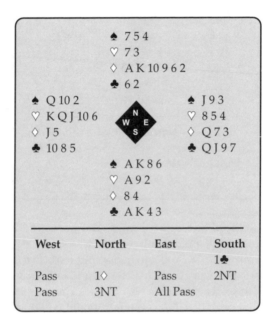

	♠ 7 5 4	
	♡ 7 3	
	◇ A K 10 9 6 2	
	♣ 6 2	
♠ Q 10 2		♠ J 9 3
♡ K Q J 10 6		♡ 8 5 4
◇ J 5		◇ Q 7 3
♣ 10 8 5		♣ Q J 9 7
	♠ A K 8 6	
	♡ A 9 2	
	◇ 8 4	
	♣ A K 4 3	

West	North	East	South
			1♣
Pass	1◇	Pass	2NT
Pass	3NT	All Pass	

Sitting West, you lead the ♡K. Declarer holds up the ♡A until the third round and leads a low diamond from his hand. How will you defend?

If you play low, as many defenders would, declarer will finesse dummy's ◇10. Your partner wins with the ◇Q but, after declarer's hold-up in hearts, has no heart to return. Declarer can win whatever else East returns and score five diamond tricks, making the game with an overtrick.

To prevent declarer ducking the first round of diamonds into the safe hand, you should rise with the ◊J. Declarer cannot afford to play low from dummy or you will beat the game by cashing two heart winners. He wins with dummy's ◊A and cannot then enjoy more than two diamond tricks. He may decide to play you for ◊Q-J-x, returning to his hand in one of the black suits to finesse the ◊10 on the second round. If he follows this line he will score only one diamond trick!

Here is another example of this style of defence:

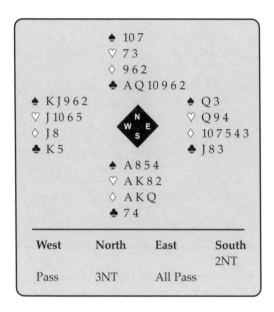

| ♠ 10 7 |
| ♡ 7 3 |
| ◊ 9 6 2 |
| ♣ A Q 10 9 6 2 |

♠ K J 9 6 2   ♠ Q 3
♡ J 10 6 5   ♡ Q 9 4
◊ J 8   ◊ 10 7 5 4 3
♣ K 5   ♣ J 8 3

♠ A 8 5 4
♡ A K 8 2
◊ A K Q
♣ 7 4

West	North	East	South
			2NT
Pass	3NT	All Pass	

Sitting West, you lead the ♠6. East produces a welcome ♠Q and declarer allows this card to win. East returns the ♠3 and you win with the ♠J, returning the ♠K to clear the suit. Declarer wins the third spade with the ace and leads the ♣4 towards dummy. How will you defend?

Play the ♣5 and declarer will not be troubled. 'Ten, please,' he will say. Your partner will win with the ♣J but will have no spade to return. Declarer can capture the red-suit exit and lead another club, intending to finesse the queen. The appearance of your ♣K will spare him this task and he will make an overtrick.

As you see, life will not be so enjoyable for declarer if you rise with the ♣K on the first round. He cannot afford to duck or you will cash two more spades. He wins with dummy's ♣A, therefore, and cannot now make more than two club tricks. If he crosses to his hand and finesses the

♣10 on the second round, playing you for ♣K-J-5, he will score only one club trick. Of course, there is nothing to be lost by rising with the ♣K in this way. The king, under dummy's ace-queen, was dead meat anyway.

Even when your top card is not especially high, it can be effective to play it on the first round. Take the West cards here:

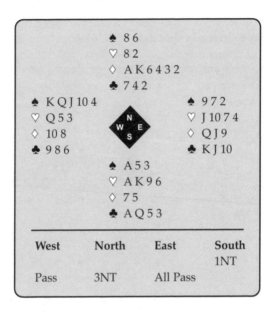

♠ 8 6			
♡ 8 2			
◇ A K 6 4 3 2			
♣ 7 4 2			

```
               ♠ 8 6
               ♡ 8 2
               ◇ A K 6 4 3 2
               ♣ 7 4 2
  ♠ K Q J 10 4          ♠ 9 7 2
  ♡ Q 5 3               ♡ J 10 7 4
  ◇ 10 8                ◇ Q J 9
  ♣ 9 8 6               ♣ K J 10
               ♠ A 5 3
               ♡ A K 9 6
               ◇ 7 5
               ♣ A Q 5 3
```

West	North	East	South
			1NT
Pass	3NT	All Pass	

You lead the ♠K and persist with spades, declarer winning the third round. How will you defend when the ◇5 is led to the fourth trick?

It may not seem to make much difference whether you play the ◇8 or the ◇10. Think again! If you follow with the ◇8, declarer's eyes will light up. From his point of view this is the lowest spot-card not on display. He can duck with confidence, forcing East (the safe hand) to overtake. Since East has no spade to return, declarer will make the game easily.

Follow the present Tip, rising with the ◇10 on the first round, and you will wipe the smile from declarer's face. If he ducks, you will cash two more spades to beat the game. If instead he wins, dummy's diamond suit will be dead. With only two diamond tricks at his disposal he will go down, despite the very favourable club position.

Combine your chances in the right order

If you can combine two chances to make the contract, this is nearly always better than relying on just one chance. It is often the case, though, that you must take your chances in the right order. Ask yourself 'If my first chance fails, will the defenders be able to stop me using the second chance?' It's not an easy situation to visualize, you're right, so let's see an example straight away:

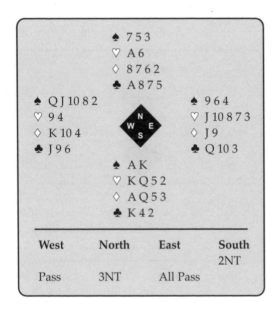

	♠ 7 5 3	
	♡ A 6	
	◇ 8 7 6 2	
	♣ A 8 7 5	
♠ Q J 10 8 2		♠ 9 6 4
♡ 9 4		♡ J 10 8 7 3
◇ K 10 4		◇ J 9
♣ J 9 6		♣ Q 10 3
	♠ A K	
	♡ K Q 5 2	
	◇ A Q 5 3	
	♣ K 4 2	

West	North	East	South
			2NT
Pass	3NT	All Pass	

West leads the ♠Q against your contract of 3NT and you win in the South hand. How will you play the contract?

You have eight tricks on top and a successful diamond finesse will bring your total to nine. Another possibility is to find the clubs breaking 3-3, which will allow you to set up a third trick in the suit. How can you combine these two chances?

Suppose you cross to dummy with the ♡A, and finesse the ◇Q. West will win and clear the spade suit. It will then be too late to concede a club trick, hoping for a 3-3 break in the suit. If you did, the defenders would cash three spade tricks, putting you one down.

To benefit from both chances you must play clubs first, surrendering a trick there while you still have a spade stopper. After winning the spade lead you should cash the ace and king of clubs and then play a third round of clubs. When the cards lie as in the diagram, the suit breaks 3-3 and you have your ninth trick. If clubs are not 3-3, nothing has been lost. You can win the defenders' spade return and cross to the ♡A to take your second chance, the diamond finesse. You will make the contract when clubs are 3-3 or East holds the ◇K.

What was the point to remember about the last deal? You played on clubs first because that was the suit where you would have to surrender a trick. The next deal follows the same theme, although both chances involve taking a finesse.

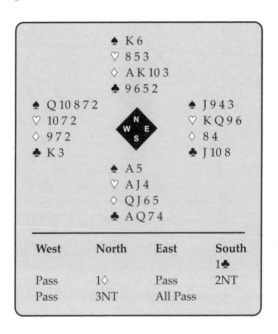

	♠ K 6	
	♡ 853	
	◇ A K 10 3	
	♣ 9 6 5 2	

♠ Q 10 8 7 2		♠ J 9 4 3
♡ 10 7 2		♡ K Q 9 6
◇ 9 7 2		◇ 8 4
♣ K 3		♣ J 10 8

	♠ A 5	
	♡ A J 4	
	◇ Q J 6 5	
	♣ A Q 7 4	

West	North	East	South
			1♣
Pass	1◇	Pass	2NT
Pass	3NT	All Pass	

How will you play 3NT when West leads the ♠7? As on the previous deal, you have eight top tricks. A successful club finesse will give you a ninth trick. A less obvious chance of a ninth trick is to find East with both the king and queen of hearts, which will allow you to set up your ♡J. How should you combine these two chances?

You cannot establish the ♡J without surrendering the lead, so this is the suit that you should play first. Win the spade lead with dummy's king and lead a low heart. If East plays low, you will finesse the ♡J, scoring your extra trick immediately. Suppose East rises with the ♡K instead. You win with the ♡A, return to dummy with a diamond and lead a second round of hearts towards the ♡J. Again a ninth trick will be yours.

If no luck comes from the hearts, nothing will be lost. When the defenders clear the spade suit, you will return to dummy with a diamond and take the club finesse. By combining your chances in this way, you will make the contract when East holds the ♣K or the ♡K-Q.

There is space left on the page, so let's tweak that last deal a bit:

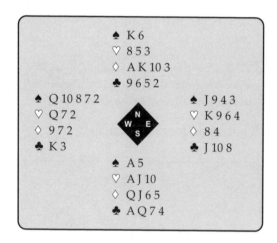

Only the hearts have changed. How will you play 3NT when the ♠7 is led?

You win with the ♠K and play a heart to the jack, which will be an immediate success when East holds the king-queen of hearts. The finesse loses to the queen and West clears the spades. What next?

A finesse of the ♣Q is a 50% chance, although you can improve on that slightly by cashing the ♡A first in case the ♡K falls doubleton. A finesse of the ♡10 is much better than that. It is around a 68% prospect, since it will lose only when West began with both heart honours. (This is an example of Restricted Choice. It is more likely that West won with the ♡Q because he had to, rather than because he chose it from the ♡K-Q).

Tip 14

Bid 5NT to invite a grand slam

In rubber bridge it is normal for 4NT to be simple Blackwood, asking for aces. In tournament bridge, many players prefer Roman Key-card Blackwood, where the responses indicate also whether the trump king and queen are held. In both cases a continuation of 5NT asks partner for side-suit kings, although there are two methods of responding. You can either give a count of kings or cue-bid the cheapest king that you hold.

That is only half the story, though. A continuation of 5NT also passes an important message: 'We hold all the key cards, partner. If you have an extra source of tricks, leap directly to the grand slam.'

Let's see an example of the 5NT bid in action:

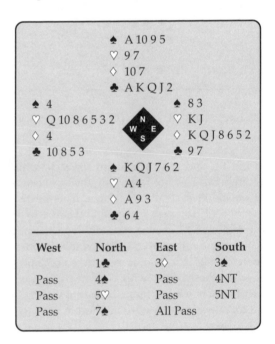

	♠ A 10 9 5		
	♡ 9 7		
	◊ 10 7		
	♣ A K Q J 2		

♠ 4			♠ 8 3
♡ Q 10 8 6 5 3 2			♡ K J
◊ 4			◊ K Q J 8 6 5 2
♣ 10 8 5 3			♣ 9 7

	♠ K Q J 7 6 2
	♡ A 4
	◊ A 9 3
	♣ 6 4

West	North	East	South
	1♣	3◊	3♠
Pass	4♠	Pass	4NT
Pass	5♡	Pass	5NT
Pass	7♠	All Pass	

On this particular deal North would respond 5♡ whether traditional or Roman Key-card Blackwood was being used. Since all the key cards are present, and a grand slam is still possible, South continues with 5NT. It is not so much that he will be able to bid a grand slam, even if North shows two side-suit kings. The point is that North may be able to diagnose a grand slam, once he knows that all the aces and the king-queen of trumps are present. Here North has a fine club suit, which will provide several extra tricks. Rather than show one side-suit king (when South would sign off in 6♠), North leaps directly to the grand slam, which is easily made.

Let's see what can go wrong when a player decides not to follow the 4NT-5NT route.

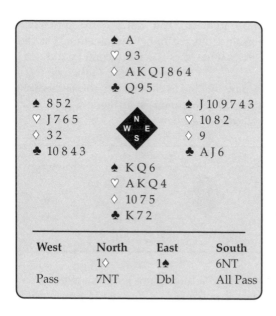

West	North	East	South
	1◊	1♠	6NT
Pass	7NT	Dbl	All Pass

The deal comes from the 2005 African Zonal Championships, with Kenya facing the eventual winners, Egypt. East overcalled in spades and South decided to attempt 6NT. You may reckon that this is a slight overbid but a reasonable gamble. Think again! Just look at the problem that the immediate 6NT bid caused poor North. Not only did he have the ace of the enemy suit, he also held seven running tricks in diamonds. He surely cannot be faulted for his decision to bid 7NT and the Kenyans arrived in a grand slam with an ace missing.

The problem was caused because North had a substantial source of extra tricks but did not know if all the aces were present. This is how the bidding should have gone, using Roman Key-card Blackwood:

West	North	East	South
	1♢	1♠	4NT
Pass	5♣	Pass	6NT
All Pass			

North's 5♣ would show three key-cards (♢A, ♢K and ♣A). Knowing that a key-card was missing, South would not continue with 5NT. He would sign off in 6NT. North would not then be invited to bid a grand slam with extra playing strength. He would have to trust his partner and pass. (Playing simple Blackwood, North would respond 5♡ and again pass partner's sign-off in 6NT.) You can see the difference between the original auction and the recommended auction. On the first auction, North had to guess what to do; on the second he did not.

Let's end the Tip by looking at another situation where responder has to recognise the failure of his partner to invite a grand slam by bidding 5NT. Suppose you are West here:

♠ A Q 10 3		♠ K J 8 7 2	West	East
♡ 7 2		♡ K Q 10 9 4 3	1♢	1♡
♢ A K Q 10 5		♢ 2	1♠	4NT
♣ K 3		♣ A	5♠	6♠
			?	

Sitting West, you hold a huge hand for your bidding and may suspect that a grand slam is possible. You must trust your partner, however. He knows that your hand is relatively unlimited. If all the key cards were present, he would have bid 5NT to tell you this. The fact that he has bid a small slam instead indicates that a key card is missing. You must grit your teeth and pass.

Tip
15

Establish a discard before drawing trumps

There are several reasons why it may not be right to draw trumps straight away. One of them is that you need to establish a discard for one of your side-suit losers. If you play a trump straight away, allowing a defender to win the lead, he may attack the suit where you hold the loser. This is a straightforward example:

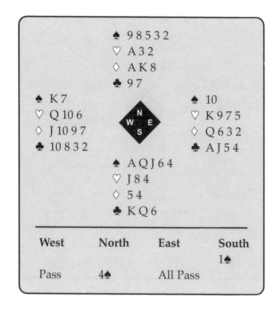

```
              ♠ 9 8 5 3 2
              ♡ A 3 2
              ◇ A K 8
              ♣ 9 7
♠ K 7                          ♠ 10
♡ Q 10 6          N            ♡ K 9 7 5
◇ J 10 9 7    W       E        ◇ Q 6 3 2
♣ 10 8 3 2        S            ♣ A J 5 4
              ♠ A Q J 6 4
              ♡ J 8 4
              ◇ 5 4
              ♣ K Q 6
```

West	North	East	South
			1♠
Pass	4♠	All Pass	

How will you play 4♠ when West leads the ◇J, won in the dummy?

If your next move is to lead a trump, you risk going down. When West wins with the ♠K he may well switch to the ♡6, seeking a trick or two in that suit. You will then lose two heart tricks, putting you one down. Instead you should lead a club towards your hand at trick two, hoping to find the ♣A onside and set up a discard.

If East plays low, you will win with the ♣K. You then cross to dummy with the remaining diamond honour and lead another club. Let's say that East rises with the ♣A and switches to the ♡5. West will cover whatever card you play from the South hand. You win with dummy's

---

♡A and cross to the ♠A, rightly spurning the chance to finesse in the suit. You can then discard one of dummy's remaining hearts on the ♣Q. You lose just one trump, one heart and one club.

You would make the same play (a club at trick two) even if your trumps were stronger, something like ♠A-K-10-6-4. If the defenders' trumps broke 3-0, you would then avoid defeat when the ♣A was onside.

Sometimes you have two stoppers in the side suit where a potential loser is lurking, but one has been removed by the opening lead. Again it may be right to seek to set up a discard. Test yourself on this deal:

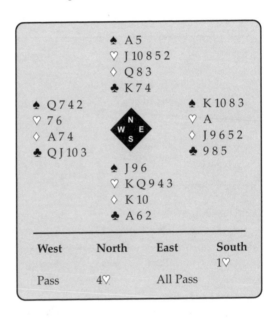

	♠ A 5	
	♡ J 10 8 5 2	
	◇ Q 8 3	
	♣ K 7 4	
♠ Q 7 4 2		♠ K 10 8 3
♡ 7 6		♡ A
◇ A 7 4		◇ J 9 6 5 2
♣ Q J 10 3		♣ 9 8 5
	♠ J 9 6	
	♡ K Q 9 4 3	
	◇ K 10	
	♣ A 6 2	

West	North	East	South
			1♡
Pass	4♡	All Pass	

West leads the ♣Q. How will you play the contract?

If you win the club lead and play a trump, you will go down. East will win and remove your last club stopper. There will then be no way to avoid a loser in every suit. Instead, you must aim to set up a club discard on the diamonds. You win the club lead with the king in dummy and lead a low diamond, finessing the ten. Fortune favours the brave on this occasion and the ◇10 forces West's ◇A.

You win the club continuation with the ace, unblock the ◇K and cross to dummy with the ♠A. You can then discard your club loser on dummy's ◇Q. Finally it is safe to play a trump and you will lose just one spade, one heart and one diamond. You risk going two down by finessing the ◇10, yes, but it is the only real chance of making the contract.

Here is another deal on the same theme:

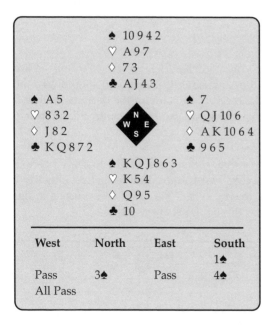

West	North	East	South
			1♠
Pass	3♠	Pass	4♠
All Pass			

How will you play 4♠ when West leads the ♣K?

You win with the ♣A. Suppose you play a trump to the king next. West will win and may switch to hearts. There will then be no way to avoid four losers. How can you dispose of your heart loser?

It is a long-shot to hope that West holds ♣K-Q-x and you can establish dummy's ♣J with a couple of ruffs. A better chance is to hope that East holds the ace and king of diamonds. (This is normally a 1-in-4 chance, but once West has not led the suit it becomes closer to a 1-in-3 chance.) So, at trick two you lead a low diamond towards your hand. East rises with the ◇K and switches to the ♡Q. You win in the dummy and lead another diamond. East wins with the ◇A and plays another heart. You win with the ♡K and discard dummy's remaining heart on the established ◇Q. Only then can you afford to play a trump.

Hold on to the ace of trumps

When you are defending, the ace of trumps is a precious asset. By thinking carefully when you should take the ace, you can make life very difficult for the declarer. In this Tip we will see some situations where you can beat a contract by holding up the ace of trumps.

It often happens that declarer would like to draw precisely two rounds of trumps, leaving one trump at large, before attempting a ruff with dummy's last trump. When you hold three trumps to the ace, you can upset declarer's timing. Look at this deal:

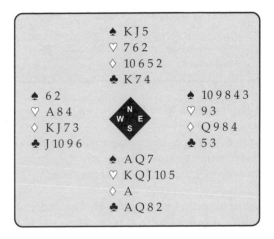

Defending 6♡ on the West cards, you lead the ♣J. Declarer wins with dummy's ♣K and plays a trump to the king. How will you defend?

Let's see what will happen if you win the first round of trumps. Declarer wins your ♣10 continuation with the ♣A and draws one more round of trumps. He then tests the club suit by playing the ♣Q. East shows out but cannot ruff because he does not hold the defenders' last trump. Declarer ruffs the fourth round of clubs in the dummy and the slam is made.

You can stop declarer from drawing precisely two rounds of trumps by holding up the ace of trumps on the first round. If he plays another trump, you will win with the ace and draw a third round, preventing a club ruff. If instead declarer plays on clubs straight away, your partner will still have a trump left and can ruff the third round of clubs.

On the next deal you must hold up the ace of trumps to prevent declarer from drawing your own last trump. Take the East cards.

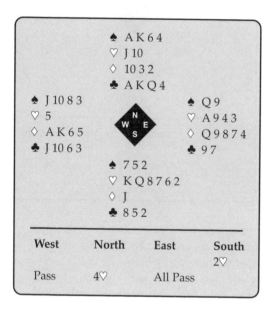

	♠ A K 6 4	
	♡ J 10	
	◇ 10 3 2	
	♣ A K Q 4	

♠ J 10 8 3		♠ Q 9
♡ 5		♡ A 9 4 3
◇ A K 6 5		◇ Q 9 8 7 4
♣ J 10 6 3		♣ 9 7

	♠ 7 5 2	
	♡ K Q 8 7 6 2	
	◇ J	
	♣ 8 5 2	

West	North	East	South
			2♡
Pass	4♡	All Pass	

West leads the ◇A and you encourage with the ◇9. Declarer ruffs the next diamond and plays a trump to the jack. How will you defend?

You should allow the ♡J to win and duck again when declarer plays the ♡10. The contract can no longer be made. If declarer reaches his hand with a diamond ruff to lead the ♡K, you will win and force his last trump with another diamond. The ♡9 and a diamond will then beat the contract.

When dummy holds only two trumps and you have a doubleton ace in the suit, it can be effective to lead a low trump at some stage. Your idea will be to cash some winners when you eventually take the trump ace. Let's see an example of that.

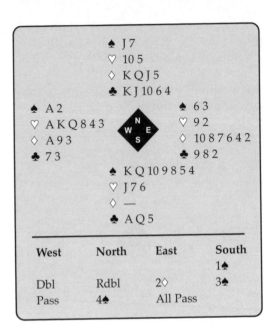

	♠ J 7		
	♡ 10 5		
	◇ K Q J 5		
	♣ K J 10 6 4		

West		East
♠ A 2		♠ 6 3
♡ A K Q 8 4 3		♡ 9 2
◇ A 9 3		◇ 10 8 7 6 4 2
♣ 7 3		♣ 9 8 2

	♠ K Q 10 9 8 5 4
	♡ J 7 6
	◇ —
	♣ A Q 5

West	North	East	South
			1♠
Dbl	Rdbl	2◇	3♠
Pass	4♠	All Pass	

Sitting West, you lead the ♡K against South's spade game. You are playing 'ace for attitude, king for count' opening leads, so the lead of a king asks partner to show you whether he holds an even or odd number of cards in the suit. East follows with the ♡9, which is very likely to be from a doubleton. How will you continue the defence?

Declarer has three hearts and your worry is that he will be able to ruff the third round of hearts in the dummy, with East unable to overruff the jack of trumps. How can you prevent this?

Suppose you play ace and another trump. That's no good. With the trumps drawn, declarer will simply run dummy's club suit, scoring an overtrick. The solution is a surprising one. You must lead a low trump at trick two, retaining the ace of trumps.

What can declarer do? If he plays a second round of trumps, you will win with the ace and cash two more heart tricks. No doubt declarer will play on clubs instead. Now comes a second test for you. If you ruff the third round of clubs with the ♠A, you will have no way to remove dummy's last trump and declarer will enjoy a heart ruff. No, you must discard and wait for partner to ruff the fourth round of clubs. Declarer can overruff but he will never get back to the dummy. If he plays a heart, you will win, draw dummy's last trump and cash a third heart trick for the defence.

Another 52 Great Bridge Tips

Tip
17

Block the defenders' suit

By wielding your honours to maximum effect, it is sometimes possible to block the suit that the defenders have led. Test yourself here:

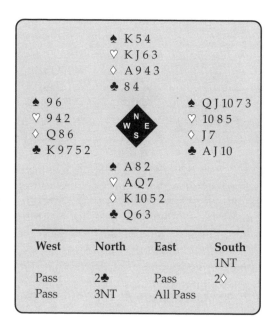

```
                    ♠ K 5 4
                    ♡ K J 6 3
                    ◇ A 9 4 3
                    ♣ 8 4
  ♠ 9 6                          ♠ Q J 10 7 3
  ♡ 9 4 2            N           ♡ 10 8 5
  ◇ Q 8 6        W     E         ◇ J 7
  ♣ K 9 7 5 2        S           ♣ A J 10
                    ♠ A 8 2
                    ♡ A Q 7
                    ◇ K 10 5 2
                    ♣ Q 6 3
```

West	North	East	South
			1NT
Pass	2♣	Pass	2◇
Pass	3NT	All Pass	

West leads the ♣5, East winning with the ♣A and returning the ♣J. How will you plan the play?

If East started with ♣A-J doubleton, you need to play low on the second round of clubs. West could not overtake with the ♣K or your ♣Q would become good. Left on lead, East would have to switch to a different suit and you would have time to develop nine tricks. East cannot hold a doubleton club, though. West's fourth-best lead of the ♣5, with only one lower spot-card not on view, proclaims at most a five-card suit. Your best chance of avoiding the immediate loss of five club tricks is to cover the ♣J with the ♣Q. West wins with the ♣K but the defenders' clubs are then blocked. West can cross to his partner's bare ♣10 but East will then have to switch. How will you continue the play when East switches to the ♠Q?

You have eight top tricks and must develop a ninth trick with letting West on lead. You should win with the ♠A and play a diamond to the nine. East wins with the ◊J and you now have an extra diamond trick, giving you the game. This play would succeed also against ◊Q-J-x-x with East. You would win East's spade continuation and cash the ◊A, setting up a finesse position against East's remaining ◊Q-x.

Here is a second deal on the same theme:

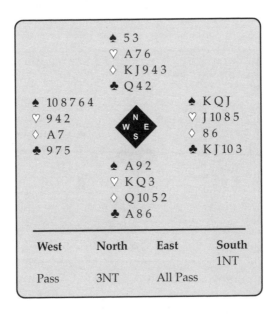

West leads the ♠6 and East plays the ♠J. How will you play the contract?

Other things being equal, this type of hand is simple to play. You plan to hold up the ♠A until the third round and then play on diamonds. You would make the contract when spades were 4-4, and posed no threat, or when West held five spades but the ◊A lay in the safe East hand. So, you allow the ♠J to win. East continues with the ♠K. What now?

If you sleepily hold up the ♠A for another round, you will go down. East will clear the spades and when you play on diamonds West will pounce with the ◊A and cash two more spades. Look again at the cards that East has played – the ♠J followed by the ♠K. This implies that he holds the ♠Q as well, since with ♠K-J-x he would have played the king on the first round. You should therefore win the second spade trick. This leaves the spade suit blocked, with East holding the bare ♠Q. When you play on diamonds, West will have to win the first or second round. The defenders cannot untangle their spade tricks and the contract will be yours. (If West held ◊A-x-x instead, he could hold up the ace for one round, allowing East to discard the blocking ♠Q on the second round of diamonds.)

An interesting point comes to mind on this deal. If East realises that you may diagnose a potential blockage in the spade suit, he should play the ♠Q on the first round, continuing with the ♠K. You are then likely to place him with ♠K-Q-x and hold up the ♠A until the third round!

Opportunities for blocking plays are common when your RHO holds only two cards in the suit led. You can often diagnose a doubleton honour because otherwise the opening leader would have held a sequence.

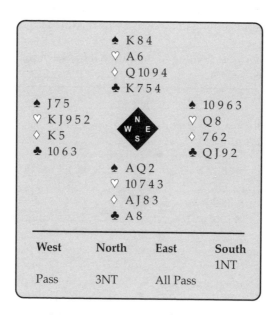

	♠ K 8 4		
	♡ A 6		
	◊ Q 10 9 4		
	♣ K 7 5 4		

♠ J 7 5		♠ 10 9 6 3
♡ K J 9 5 2		♡ Q 8
◊ K 5		◊ 7 6 2
♣ 10 6 3		♣ Q J 9 2

	♠ A Q 2		
	♡ 10 7 4 3		
	◊ A J 8 3		
	♣ A 8		

West	North	East	South
			1NT
Pass	3NT	All Pass	

How will you play 3NT when West leads the ♡5?

You have seven top tricks and can create at least two more in diamonds. The only risk is that you will lose one diamond and four hearts. Suppose you play low at trick one. East wins with the ♡Q and clears the hearts. When the diamond finesse fails, West will cash three more heart tricks to put you one down. You could guard against a singleton ◊K with West by playing ace and another diamond (since you don't mind losing a diamond trick to East), but the result would be the same.

Look back to trick one. If West's hearts were headed by the K-Q-J he would surely have led an honour, rather than the ♡5. So, it is almost certain that East holds a doubleton honour in the dangerous case where hearts break 5-2. You should rise with dummy's ♡A and the defenders will be powerless. If East unblocks the queen under dummy's ace, your remaining ♡10-7-4 will act as a stopper with West on lead. If instead East retains the ♡Q, this will block the defenders' suit.

Rising with dummy's ace was clear-cut because the diamond finesse was into the West hand. Suppose we swap the North-South diamond holdings and give East the ◊K. Rising with the ♡A on the first round would then cost you the contract. East would unblock the ♡Q under dummy's ace. When the diamond finesse subsequently lost to his king, he would return the ♡8 through your ♡10-7-4. With that lie of the diamond suit, you would have to play differently. You would hold up the ♡A for one round, aiming to exhaust East's holding in the suit.

Let's strengthen your holding in the suit that has been led:

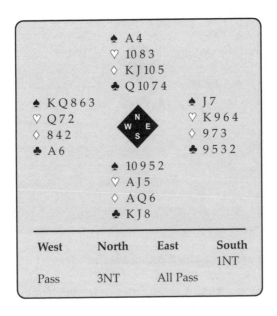

West	North	East	South
			1NT
Pass	3NT	All Pass	

How will you play 3NT when West leads the ♣6?

Since West has not led the ♠K, you can place East with a doubleton honour in the dangerous 5-2 case. You with the ♠A at trick one and will then be safe whoever holds the ♣A. Your ♠10-9-5 will stop the suit from either side of the table.

Tip 18

Respond in the longer suit when strong

Your partner opens 1♡ and the next player passes. How would you respond on these two hands?

	(1)		(2)
♠	K 10 7 2	♠	A J 10 2
♡	7	♡	6 2
◇	J 8 4	◇	7 3
♣	A 9 8 5 2	♣	A K 8 7 2

There is no problem on hand (1). Since you are not strong enough to bid at the two-level, whether you play Acol or Standard American, you must respond 1♠. What about hand (2), though? You will see many players who respond 1♠ on this hand too. "A response of 2♣ would deny four spades," they say. What nonsense!

When you are strong enough to make two bids, in other words when you hold 11 points or more, you should respond in the longer suit. You intend to bid the spades on the next round, if appropriate. This is a likely start to the auction:

West	East
1♡	2♣
2♡	2♠

What could be more satisfactory? You have shown that you hold the values for a game try, at least, and you have bid your suits in the right order – the longer suit first.

If you feel obliged to mention the four-card spade suit with your first response, you will be forced into this less satisfactory start to the auction:

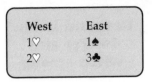

West	East
1♡	1♠
2♡	3♣

Not so good, is it? Not only has the bidding been carried to a higher level, you have also given partner a false impression of your black-suit lengths. What on earth are you going to bid next if partner bids 3♠, showing three-card spade support?

If you play Acol with a weak 1NT, you sometimes have to respond at the two-level (like it or not) with as little as a good nine-count or a moderate ten-count. Suppose partner opens 1♠ and you hold this hand:

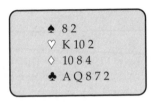

♠ 8 2
♡ K 10 2
♢ 10 8 4
♣ A Q 8 7 2

It's risky to respond 1NT because partner will pass when he holds a flat 15 or 16 points and you may miss a sound 3NT. (When the opener holds 17 points, he may raise a 1NT response to 2NT.) You have to stretch to a 2♣ response, intending to raise a 2NT rebid (15+ points) to 3NT.

When you play a weak 1NT, a two-level response may be based on only 9 or 10 points. However, that does not mean that you will necessarily respond in your longer suit. Suppose you are sitting East with this hand:

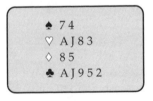

♠ 7 4
♡ A J 8 3
♢ 8 5
♣ A J 9 5 2

If partner opens 1♠, you will have to respond 2♣. Suppose instead that partner opens 1♢. You are not strong enough to make two bids. If you decided to respond 2♣ and partner rebid 2♢, you would have to pass and a possible heart fit might have been lost. So, the correct response is 1♡, which will allow a heart fit to come to light.

**Assume the lie
of the cards
that you need**

On many contracts you have to assume a particular lie in one suit for success to be possible. Even if this lie is against the odds, you must go ahead and make the necessary assumption. Look at this deal:

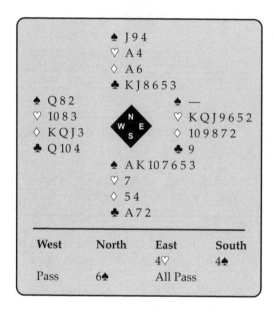

	♠ J 9 4	
	♡ A 4	
	◊ A 6	
	♣ K J 8 6 5 3	

♠ Q 8 2		♠ —
♡ 10 8 3		♡ K Q J 9 6 5 2
◊ K Q J 3		◊ 10 9 8 7 2
♣ Q 10 4		♣ 9

	♠ A K 10 7 6 5 3	
	♡ 7	
	◊ 5 4	
	♣ A 7 2	

West	North	East	South
		4♡	4♠
Pass	6♣	All Pass	

You win the ◊K lead in dummy, play a trump and... East shows out! That's unfair. How will you attempt to rectify the situation?

With a certain trump loser, you must dispose of your potential loser in diamonds. You will have to discard it on dummy's clubs and this can be done only when West holds three (or four) clubs. It would be no use playing the ♣A-K and finding the suit breaking 2-2. West would then ruff the third round of clubs before you could discard your diamond loser.

You draw two rounds of trumps and cash the ♣A, everyone following. Your only chance now is to finesse dummy's ♣J. The finesse wins, as it happens, you cash the ♣K and continue with a good club, throwing your diamond loser. West can score his ♠Q when he likes. The slam is yours.

It's rather strange but if West had made a seemingly ineffective heart lead you might have gone down. Since there would be no need to place West with three clubs, you would have a losing alternative of playing for a 2-2 club break! Here is a more difficult deal on the same theme:

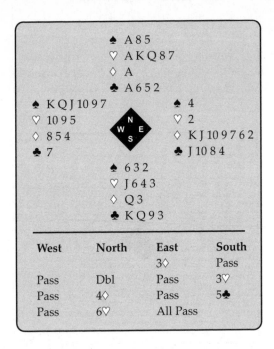

West	North	East	South
		3◇	Pass
Pass	Dbl	Pass	3♡
Pass	4◇	Pass	5♣
Pass	6♡	All Pass	

West leads the ♠K and your first inspection of the dummy is not reassuring. Can you see *any* way that the contract may be made?

If East began with a singleton spade, an elimination play is possible. You would draw trumps, eliminate the club suit, and throw East on lead with the ◇Q to his ◇K, discarding a spade from dummy. East's enforced diamond return would then concede a ruff-and-discard, allowing you to ruff in the South hand and discard the last spade from dummy.

When you draw trumps, East turns up with only one card in the suit. Since you need him to have started with just one spade, his shape will have to be 1-1-7-4. You play the ♣A, dropping the ♣7 from West and the ♣4 from East. Since you need East to hold four clubs for the contract to be made, you must now finesse the ♣9! When the finesse succeeds, West showing out, you cross to the ◇A and play the ♣K-Q. The lead is in the South hand in this end position:

Another 52 Great Bridge Tips

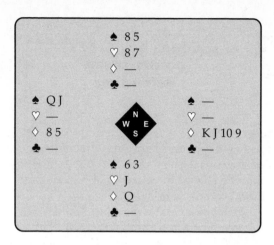

You exit with the ◊Q, throwing a spade from dummy. East wins with the ◊K and is indeed forced to give you a ruff-and-discard. A long journey, yes, but the effort was worthwhile. The slam is now yours.

Tip 20

Count declarer's points when defending

Whenever you are defending and declarer has given a close count of his points, by opening or rebidding in notrumps, you should watch the high cards that he produces. By counting his points, you may be able to work out what honour cards your partner holds. Take the West cards here:

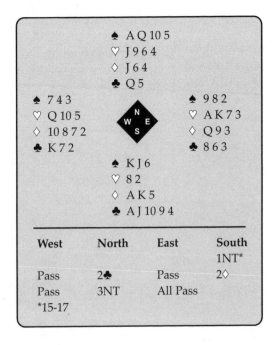

```
               ♠ A Q 10 5
               ♡ J 9 6 4
               ◊ J 6 4
               ♣ Q 5
 ♠ 7 4 3                      ♠ 9 8 2
 ♡ Q 10 5       N            ♡ A K 7 3
 ◊ 10 8 7 2   W   E          ◊ Q 9 3
 ♣ K 7 2        S            ♣ 8 6 3
               ♠ K J 6
               ♡ 8 2
               ◊ A K 5
               ♣ A J 10 9 4
```

West	North	East	South
			1NT*
Pass	2♣	Pass	2◊
Pass	3NT	All Pass	
*15-17			

You lead the ◊2 against 3NT and dummy's ◊J is covered by East's ◊Q and declarer's ◊K. The ♣6 is led to dummy's ♣Q and declarer then runs the ♣Q. How will you defend in the West seat?

Only three tricks have been played but already you can place several honours in the South hand. Dummy's ♠Q won the first round of spades, so South is likely to hold the ♠K. You know he holds the ◊A-K and the play in clubs makes sense only if he holds ♣A-J as well. (If your partner held the ♣A, he would doubtless have won the first round of the suit and returned a diamond.) Add up the points South has already shown and the total comes to 15. You can therefore deduce that your partner must hold the ace and king of hearts. To beat the contract, he will need to hold ♡A-K-8-x or ♡A-K-7-x. Can you see which heart you should switch to?

You must switch to the ♡10, covered by the jack and king. East can then return the ♡3 to your ♡Q. Thanks to your unblock of the ♡10, you can now lead the ♡5 through dummy's ♡9-6 to partner's awaiting ♡A-7. You may think that the heart unblocking play was rather fancy. Yes, but the main point of the hand is that you could place partner with the ♡A-K because you had taken the trouble to count declarer's points.

Stay in the West seat as you tackle the defence on this deal:

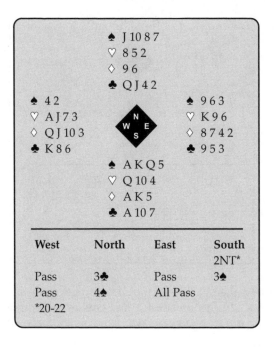

	♠ J 10 8 7	
	♡ 8 5 2	
	◊ 9 6	
	♣ Q J 4 2	

♠ 4 2		♠ 9 6 3
♡ A J 7 3		♡ K 9 6
◊ Q J 10 3		◊ 8 7 4 2
♣ K 8 6		♣ 9 5 3

	♠ A K Q 5	
	♡ Q 10 4	
	◊ A K 5	
	♣ A 10 7	

West	North	East	South
			2NT*
Pass	3♣	Pass	3♠
Pass	4♠	All Pass	
*20-22			

You lead the ◊Q against 4♠, East producing a discouraging ◊2. Declarer wins, cashes the ace and king of trumps and leads a low trump to dummy's jack, partner following three times. The ♣Q is then run to your ♣K, partner following with the ♣3. How will you defend?

How many points has South shown? He holds the ♠A-K-Q, the ◊A-K (when partner's discouraging signal is taken into account) and is very likely to hold the ♣A, to explain his play in clubs. That is 20 points outside hearts. Since the ♡K would carry him past the 22-point maximum for 2NT, you can place that card with your partner. So, you win with the ♣K and switch to the ♡3. East wins with the ♡K and returns the ♡9, allowing the defence to score three heart tricks. That is one down.

If you had failed to take three heart tricks, perhaps continuing with the ◊J, declarer would have thrown a heart loser on the dummy's long club.

Let's alter that deal a bit and see how, with different evidence, you might choose to defend more passively:

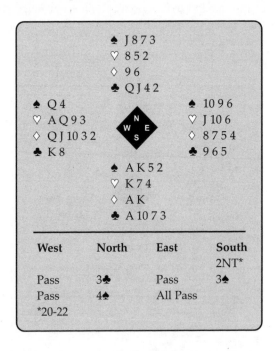

West	North	East	South
			2NT*
Pass	3♣	Pass	3♠
Pass	4♠	All Pass	
*20-22			

Again you lead the ◊Q and partner discourages with the ◊4. Declarer plays the ♠A-K, dropping your ♠Q, and crosses to dummy with the ♠J. Once more the ♣Q is run to your ♣K. How do you defend?

Making the same assumptions as before, you count South for 18 points outside hearts. He must therefore hold the ♡K. This time it cannot be right to switch to the ♡3, hoping that East holds the ♡K and the defenders can cash three heart tricks. So, exit passively with a club or a diamond. Declarer will cash his remaining winners in the minor suits and eventually lead a heart from dummy, hoping to duck the trick to you in the West seat (leaving you end-played). Provided your partner is awake, he will rise with the ♡J or ♡10 when the heart is led from dummy. The defenders will then score three heart tricks to defeat the game.

Tip
21

**Preserve the
high trump to
avoid an overruff**

W hen the deal below arose at the table, declarer was busy congratulating himself for the excellence of his bidding and could not imagine that he would go down. A few moments later he was writing a minus score on his card. See if you could have avoided his mistake.

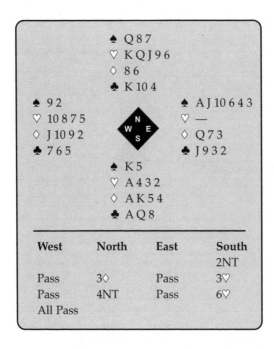

North indicated five hearts with his transfer response of 3◊ and then suggested a slam with his limit rebid of 4NT. (It makes good sense to play 4NT as a limit bid after Stayman or a transfer response – two Tips for the price of one here!) With excellent heart support South leapt to a small slam in that suit. How would you play 6♡ when West leads the ◊J?

Declarer won the first trick with the ◊A. There seemed to be just one potential loser, in spades, so without further thought he played the ♡A. When East showed out, declarer could not draw all the trumps before taking a spade ruff. He led the ♠K, East winning with the ♠A and

---

returning a diamond. Declarer won with the ◇K, crossed to the ♣Q and ruffed a spade. Disaster! West overruffed and that was one down.

When a contract appears to be cold, you must think of the distribution that might defeat you. Here the risk was that a defender might hold four trumps, preventing declarer from drawing trumps before seeking a spade ruff, and that the same defender would also hold a doubleton spade. Declarer should have played a trump to the king at trick two, retaining the ♡A. He could then give up a spade and ruff the third round of spades with the ♡A, avoiding any risk of an overruff. The marked finesse of the ♡9 would allow him to draw trumps and claim the contract.

Declarer made a similar mistake on this deal:

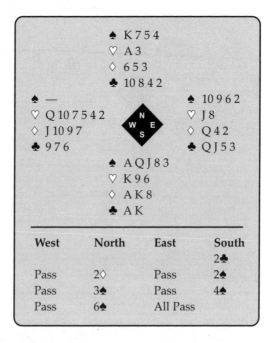

West	North	East	South
			2♣
Pass	2◇	Pass	2♠
Pass	3♠	Pass	4♠
Pass	6♠	All Pass	

How will you play the slam when West leads the ◇J?

Concluding that the contract was cold, declarer won with the ◇A and played a trump to the king. The slam could no longer be made! There was no way to avoid a diamond loser and declarer was overruffed when he tried to ruff a heart. 'Not my lucky day!' he exclaimed.

A 4-0 trump break was the only potential problem. After winning the diamond lead, you should play the ♠A. When West shows out, you cross to the ♡A to lead a second trump from the table. If East plays low, you will finesse the ♠8. Let's assume that East inserts the ♠10 and you win with the ♠Q. You cash the ♡K and ruff a heart with the ♠K. You can then finesse the ♠8, draw East's last trump with the ♠J and the slam is yours.

We will end the Tip with a different type of hand, one where you are missing a trump honour and have the option of finessing against it.

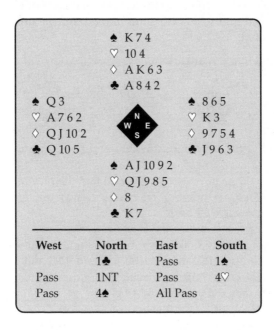

	♠ K 7 4	
	♡ 10 4	
	◇ A K 6 3	
	♣ A 8 4 2	

♠ Q 3		♠ 8 6 5
♡ A 7 6 2		♡ K 3
◇ Q J 10 2		◇ 9 7 5 4
♣ Q 10 5		♣ J 9 6 3

	♠ A J 10 9 2	
	♡ Q J 9 8 5	
	◇ 8	
	♣ K 7	

West	North	East	South
	1♣	Pass	1♠
Pass	1NT	Pass	4♡
Pass	4♠	All Pass	

Declarer won the ◇Q lead in dummy and continued with king and another trump, finessing the jack. Retribution was swift. The bidding had placed declarer with ten cards in the major suits, so West knew there were no tricks available in the minors. He switched to a low heart and the defenders scored a heart ruff with the ♠8 to defeat the game.

How should declarer play? It is not safe to play the ♠A-K because a defender might win the third round from ♠Q-8-6-5 and again score a ruff. No, declarer should lead a low trump to the jack at trick two. West would win with the ♠Q but three rounds of hearts would then pose no threat. Declarer could ruff the third round with the ♠K and draw trumps.

Tip
22

With 19 points make a 2NT jump rebid

How should you bid when you hold a balanced hand containing 19 points? Back in the Dark Ages, players would open with a one-bid and rebid 3NT after a one-level response. This was a typical auction:

♠ K J 4		♠ Q 10 9 6 3	West	East
♡ A 5 2	N	♡ 10 7	1◇	1♠
◇ A K J 2	W E	◇ Q 7	3NT	
♣ K 10 8	S	♣ Q 9 7 4		

The game would go down on a heart lead and the players would shake their heads. 'That was unlucky. There was no way to find the 5-3 spade fit with you holding a 19-count.'

Why did West have to make such a high rebid? Because the standard system was to open 1NT with 12-14, to rebid 1NT with 15-16 and to jump-rebid 2NT with 17-18. As a result it was often difficult to find a 5-3 major suit fit when the opener held 19 points.

A much more sensible system is to open 12-14 with 1NT, to rebid 1NT on 15-17 and to jump-rebid 2NT on 18-19. If you prefer to play a strong 1NT of 15-17 points, you rebid 1NT with 12-14 and again use a jump to 2NT to show 18-19. Now the bidding goes more sweetly on the pair of hands that we just saw:

♠ K J 4		♠ Q 10 9 6 3	West	East
♡ A 5 2	N	♡ 10 7	1◇	1♠
◇ A K J 2	W E	◇ Q 7	2NT	3♠
♣ K 10 8	S	♣ Q 9 7 4	4♠	

The 2NT rebid is non-forcing, but if East makes any suit bid at the three-level (including rebidding his suit, or returning to the opener's suit) this is game-forcing. On a stronger hand with this shape, East could rebid 3♣.

Another 52 Great Bridge Tips

It would be inappropriate here because he does not want to invite club support, bypassing 3NT, when he has such a moderate hand.

If you play a four-card major system, rebidding 2NT with 19 points will allow you to find a 5-3 fit in the opener's suit too.

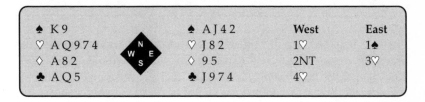

		West	East
♠ K 9	♠ A J 4 2	1♡	1♠
♡ A Q 9 7 4	♡ J 8 2	2NT	3♡
◊ A 8 2	◊ 9 5	4♡	
♣ A Q 5	♣ J 9 7 4		

If West's system forces a 3NT rebid, East would have to pass in case the heart fit was only 4-3.

Many players nowadays like to open 2NT on a 19-count. For example, if they play the Multi 2◊ they may open 2NT on 19-20. With 21-22 they open 2◊ and rebid 2NT. Or the two sequences can be reversed. As I see it, this is a poor idea. It means that you get too high when you hold 19 points and partner has a bust. Since you need partner to find a response to a one-bid before a game will be possible, it is a better tactic to open at the one-level with 19 points.

Compare these two starts to an auction:

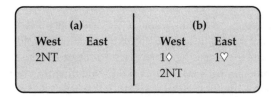

(a)		(b)	
West	East	West	East
2NT		1◊	1♡
		2NT	

Just look how much more information has been exchanged in the second auction!

Slam bidding becomes easier when you rebid 2NT on 19 points. Look at this example:

♠ A 9		♠ K Q 4 2	**West**	**East**
♡ K Q 9 7 4		♡ A 6 3	1♡	1♠
◇ A 8 2		◇ K 5	2NT	3♡
♣ A Q 5		♣ 10 8 6 3	4♣	4◇
			4♠	6♡

West cue-bids 4♣ to confirm that there is a 5-3 heart fit. (With only four hearts, he would have bid 3NT instead.) Two more cue-bids follow and East then leaps to a small slam. After the old-fashioned auction of 1♡ – 1♠ – 3NT, East would be gambling if he decided to bid again.

While we are on the subject of 2NT jump rebids, have you ever had a bidding misunderstanding after this auction:

♠ A 9 4		♠ Q 10 8 3	**West**	**East**
♡ A 10 7		♡ Q 6 4 2	1♣	1♡
◇ A 8 2		◇ K 4	2NT	3♠
♣ A Q J 5		♣ 9 7 2	?	

How many hearts do you think East shows on this auction? It seems to happen quite often that West thinks his partner has 'reversed'. Placing East with 4-5 shape in the majors, he bids 4♡ now.

There are various methods available to deal with this situation. The simplest is that East will rebid 3♡ (forcing) when he holds four spades and five hearts. West can then introduce a four-card spade suit from his side of the table. By the way, this method will allow the stronger hand to play a spade contract if there is a 4-4 fit in that suit.

Tip 23

Swap tricks to keep the danger hand off lead

Many clever moves by declarer involve keeping the dangerous defender off lead. In this Tip we will see how you can sometimes swap tricks to this effect. With that clue in mind, test yourself on the first deal:

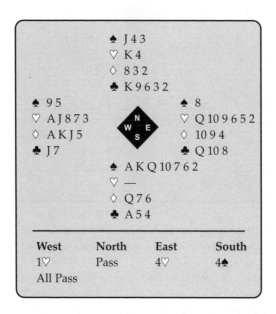

	♠ J 4 3	
	♡ K 4	
	◇ 8 3 2	
	♣ K 9 6 3 2	
♠ 9 5		♠ 8
♡ A J 8 7 3		♡ Q 10 9 6 5 2
◇ A K J 5		◇ 10 9 4
♣ J 7		♣ Q 10 8
	♠ A K Q 10 7 6 2	
	♡ —	
	◇ Q 7 6	
	♣ A 5 4	

West	North	East	South
1♡	Pass	4♡	4♠
All Pass			

West leads the ◇A and receives a discouraging ◇4 from his partner. How will you play the contract when West switches to the ♠5?

You need to set up the clubs, to throw a diamond loser. Suppose you draw trumps and play ace, king and another club. All would be well if West held three clubs. As the cards lie, East will win the third round and a switch back to diamonds will sink you. What can you do about it?

You should win the trump switch in your hand and lead the ♠6 to the ♠J (retaining your ♠2). You then lead the ♡K. When East cannot cover, you discard a club from your hand. By swapping losers in this way, you keep East off lead. The best West can do now is to prevent an overtrick by cashing his second diamond winner. If instead he exits passively with a

---

heart, you will establish the club suit with a ruff and play the ♠2 to dummy's ♠4 to enjoy two diamond discards on the long clubs.

On the next deal the chance to swap tricks comes on the very first trick.

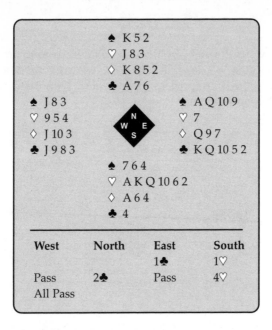

	♠ K 5 2	
	♡ J 8 3	
	◊ K 8 5 2	
	♣ A 7 6	

♠ J 8 3		♠ A Q 10 9
♡ 9 5 4		♡ 7
◊ J 10 3		◊ Q 9 7
♣ J 9 8 3		♣ K Q 10 5 2

	♠ 7 6 4	
	♡ A K Q 10 6 2	
	◊ A 6 4	
	♣ 4	

West	North	East	South
		1♣	1♡
Pass	2♣	Pass	4♡
All Pass			

'Lead me, lead me!' cried the ♠J. Not loudly enough because West led the ♣3 instead. Take the South cards. How will you play the contract?

East surely holds the ♠A and the card is unlikely to be singleton or doubleton. What other chance is there? If diamonds are 3-3, you can set up a long card there, but this must be done without allowing West (the danger hand) to gain the lead. If you simply play the ace and king of diamonds, East will have the chance to unblock the ◊Q and allow his partner to win the third round of the suit. What can be done?

You must play a low club from dummy at trick one! You are swapping a diamond loser for a club loser. East cannot play spades effectively from his side of the table. You win his return and draw two rounds of trumps with the ace and king. After playing the ace and king of diamonds, you discard your remaining diamond on the ♣A. You can then ruff a diamond high, setting up a winner in the suit. Finally, you cross to the ♡J (drawing trumps, ending in the dummy) to enjoy the long diamond.

The most famous example of this 'swapping tricks' style of play is the

Scissors Coup. It was so named by Terence Reese, because it cuts communications between the two defenders. Here is a pretty example:

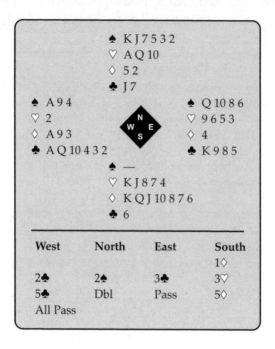

West	North	East	South
			1◇
2♣	2♠	3♣	3♡
5♣	Dbl	Pass	5◇
All Pass			

How would you play the diamond game when West leads the ♡2?

The heart lead is an obvious singleton and you can imagine what will happen if you win and play a trump. On lead with the ◇A, West will lead a low club to partner's ♣K. A heart ruff will then sink the contract. What can you do to prevent this?

You win the heart lead in the dummy and only one card is now good enough at trick two. You must lead the ♠K. East plays low and you discard your ♣6. You have swapped a club loser for a spade loser. West, the safe hand who cannot deliver a heart ruff, is on lead. You win West's return and play a trump. Since there is no longer a route to the East hand, the defenders will score just the ♠A and the ◇A. The diamond game is yours.

Tip 24

Unblock a doubleton honour in defence

Whenever declarer has plenty of trumps in both hands, there is a serious possibility that he will head for an elimination end position. What does that mean? He will eliminate the suits where you might otherwise exit safely and then throw you on lead, forcing you to give him a trick with your return. In such a situation you must be careful when you hold a doubleton honour in one of the side suits. Take the West cards here:

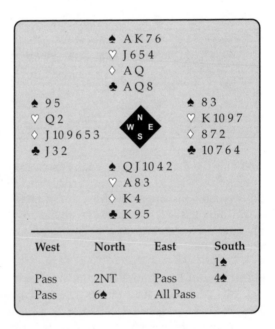

	♠ A K 7 6	
	♡ J 6 5 4	
	◊ A Q	
	♣ A Q 8	

♠ 9 5		♠ 8 3
♡ Q 2		♡ K 10 9 7
◊ J 10 9 6 5 3		◊ 8 7 2
♣ J 3 2		♣ 10 7 6 4

	♠ Q J 10 4 2	
	♡ A 8 3	
	◊ K 4	
	♣ K 9 5	

West	North	East	South
			1♠
Pass	2NT	Pass	4♠
Pass	6♠	All Pass	

Sitting West, you lead the ◊J. Declarer wins with dummy's ◊A, cashes the ♠A and leads a low heart to the ace. Do you see his cunning plan?

Suppose you follow somnolently with the ♡2. Declarer will draw the remaining trumps and cash all his winners in the minor suits. These cards will be left:

Another 52 Great Bridge Tips

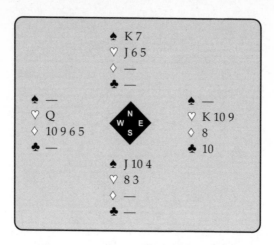

```
                    ♠ K 7
                    ♡ J 6 5
                    ◊ —
                    ♣ —
  ♠ —                              ♠ —
  ♡ Q              N               ♡ K 10 9
  ◊ 10 9 6 5    W     E            ◊ 8
  ♣ —              S               ♣ 10
                    ♠ J 10 4
                    ♡ 8 3
                    ◊ —
                    ♣ —
```

Declarer plays a heart and you are end-played with the bare ♡Q. You have to return a diamond, giving a ruff-and-discard, and declarer throws the last heart from his hand. Twelve tricks! Your partner can't overtake your ♡Q with the ♡K, of course, or dummy's ♡J will be established.

Declarer deliberately played his ♡A at an early stage, hoping that you were not alert to the elimination possibility. However, it is a clearly marked defence for you to discard the ♡Q under South's ♡A. East can then score two heart tricks with the ♡K-10 and beat the slam.

If you are nervous about 'wasting your queen', think what other heart holdings South might have. Suppose he has ♡A-10-x. He would surely have drawn trumps and played a heart to the ten, hoping to find East with a doubleton honour or both the missing honours.

Take the East cards on the next deal. Strange to relate, you have in your hand a doubleton honour. Would you have appreciated the approaching danger?

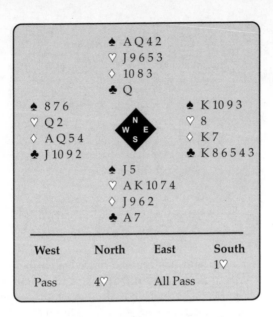

	♠ A Q 4 2		
	♡ J 9 6 5 3		
	◊ 10 8 3		
	♣ Q		

West		East
♠ 8 7 6		♠ K 10 9 3
♡ Q 2		♡ 8
◊ A Q 5 4		◊ K 7
♣ J 10 9 2		♣ K 8 6 5 4 3

	♠ J 5
	♡ A K 10 7 4
	◊ J 9 6 2
	♣ A 7

West	North	East	South
			1♡
Pass	4♡	All Pass	

Your partner leads the ♣J, covered the queen, king and ace. Declarer draws trumps in two rounds and ruffs the ♣7 in dummy. He then leads the ◊3 from the table. Well, I'm sure you remember the theme of this Tip but would you have been alert enough at the table? What is your plan for the defence?

Let's see what will happen if you play the ◊7 on the first round. West will capture South's ◊J with the ◊Q. If he returns a diamond to your king, you will be end-played – forced to lead a spade into dummy's tenace or to give a ruff-and-discard in clubs. Nor will the defence fare any better if West switches to a spade. Declarer will play low from dummy and make an easy ten tricks whether you play the ♠K or not.

So much for the impending disaster if you play low on the first round of diamonds. The time has come to see how sweetly everything will go if you bear this Tip in mind and rise with the ◊K on the first round. You return the ◊7 and your partner scores the ◊Q and the ◊A. Declarer has nowhere to park his loser in spades and the game is one down.

Another 52 Great Bridge Tips

Retain the ace as you set up a winner

Suppose you have ◇A-Q-6 in your hand and ◇J-7-5 in the dummy. You can score two diamond tricks, yes, but there are occasions when the only winning play is to lead the ◇Q from your hand. Let's see an example:

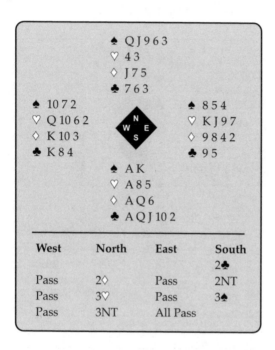

	♠ Q J 9 6 3	
	♡ 4 3	
	◇ J 7 5	
	♣ 7 6 3	
♠ 10 7 2		♠ 8 5 4
♡ Q 10 6 2	**N**	♡ K J 9 7
◇ K 10 3	**W E**	◇ 9 8 4 2
♣ K 8 4	**S**	♣ 9 5
	♠ A K	
	♡ A 8 5	
	◇ A Q 6	
	♣ A Q J 10 2	

West	North	East	South
			2♣
Pass	2◇	Pass	2NT
Pass	3♡	Pass	3♠
Pass	3NT	All Pass	

North shows five spades with a 3♡ transfer and offers a choice of games. How will you play 3NT when West leads a fourth-best ♡2 to East's ♡K?

You expect hearts to break 4-4 after the ♡2 lead but nothing can be lost by holding up the ♡A until the third round. What now? If you clear the clubs, the defenders will score four tricks and your own total will be only eight tricks. You cannot establish an extra diamond trick without giving the defence their fifth trick with the ◇K. What else can you try?

You must lead the ◇Q from your hand. If West wins with the ◇K, you will make the game easily. He cashes a heart but you will win the return,

---

unblock the spades and cross to dummy's ♢J to make three more spade tricks. Nor will West do better by ducking the ♢Q. With a diamond trick in the bag, you would establish the clubs, bringing your total to nine.

What if you unblock the ♠A-K and play the ♢A, followed by the ♢Q? It would not be good enough. West would hold up the ♢K, to keep you out of dummy. When you subsequently cleared the clubs, the defenders would have five tricks to take: three hearts, the ♢K and the ♣K. (One final point. If East switches to a club at trick two, you will go down if you finesse. You must rise with the ♣A and lead the ♢Q.)

On the next deal you retain your ace to avoid an adverse ruff.

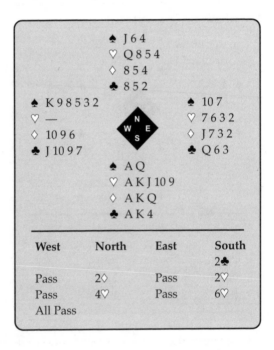

West	North	East	South
			2♣
Pass	2♢	Pass	2♡
Pass	4♡	Pass	6♡
All Pass			

West leads the ♣J, which you win with the ♣A. When you play the ace of trumps West shows out, discarding a spade. What now?

If trumps had broken 2-2 or 3-1, you would have drawn trumps and played the ace and queen of spades, setting up the spade jack and eventually reaching it with the queen of trumps. As it is, you will have to set up your spade trick before drawing all the trumps, since you need to cross to dummy with the ♡Q to enjoy the established spade trick. Suppose you draw three rounds of trumps and then play the ace and queen of spades. Not good enough! West will win and lead a third round of spades, allowing East to kill dummy's established ♠J with a ruff. You can overruff but there will then be no way to dispose of your club loser. How can you avoid this sorry outcome?

After just one or two rounds of trumps you must lead the ♠Q from your hand. West has to win, or you will have twelve tricks on top. You take his club continuation, unblock the ♠A and draw trumps, ending in the dummy. You can then enjoy a club discard on the ♠J.

There is space for one more deal, so we will look at an example of playing the queen from A-Q-J-10-3 of trumps, to control the hand.

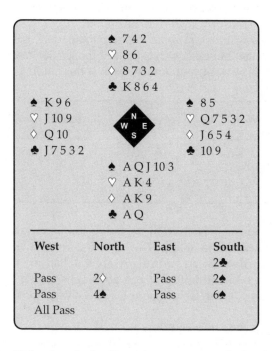

	♠ 7 4 2		
	♡ 8 6		
	◇ 8 7 3 2		
	♣ K 8 6 4		

♠ K 9 6		♠ 8 5
♡ J 10 9		♡ Q 7 5 3 2
◇ Q 10		◇ J 6 5 4
♣ J 7 5 3 2		♣ 10 9

	♠ A Q J 10 3	
	♡ A K 4	
	◇ A K 9	
	♣ A Q	

West	North	East	South
			2♣
Pass	2◇	Pass	2♠
Pass	4♠	Pass	6♠
All Pass			

You win the ♡J lead with the ♡A. Suppose you cash the ♣A-Q, reach dummy with a heart ruff and attempt to cash the ♣K. East will defeat you by ruffing. You need to draw precisely two rounds of trumps, before playing the ♣K, to reduce the risk of an adverse ruff.

Playing the ace and queen of trumps is no good because West would then return a third round of trumps. Instead you must lead the ♠Q from your hand at trick two. West wins and plays another heart. You win with the ♡K and draw a second round of trumps. After cashing the ace and queen of clubs, you enter dummy with a heart ruff. Now East has no trump with which to ruff the ♣K, so you survive.

Tip 26

Bid a suit and then double for take-out

The take-out double is one of the most useful calls in the game. In general, the more times you use the bid, the better the player you are. Less experienced players tend to bid the cards in front of them, rather than recognising the moments where it is better to show strength with a double and leave partner to choose where to play.

In this Tip we will look at some important situations where you have already bid a suit but may wish to contest the auction later. Often your best action will be a take-out double. Look at this bidding problem:

West	West	North	East	South
♠ K J 8			1♡	Pass
♡ K 6	2♣	2♢	Pass	Pass
♢ 9 5	?			
♣ A 10 9 7 6 2				

What now? You may survive by rebidding the moderate clubs but a much better action is to double. This says to partner: 'I have enough to contest the auction but no particularly accurate bid to make.' In other words, it is a take-out double. It is a good general rule that a double under the trump length (below game level) is always for take-out.

Such positions arise time and time again. If this type of double is not in your armoury, you will have to guess what to bid and will often end in the wrong contract. Here is a similar hand:

West	West	North	East	South
♠ A J 9 7 2			1♢	Pass
♡ K	1♠	2♡	Pass	Pass
♢ J 9 5	?			
♣ Q 10 8 4				

A double is best. The alternatives of 2♠, 2NT, 3♣ and 3♢ all suffer from serious flaws. The same sort of double can be made by the opener:

West	West	North	East	South
♠ A 2	1◇	1♠	2♣	Pass
♡ K 10 3	2◇	2♠	Pass	Pass
◇ A Q 10 8 7 2	?			
♣ J 3				

With 14 points facing a response at the two-level, you are unwilling to sell out. Should you bid 3♣, hoping East has a six-card suit? Should you bid your diamonds one more time? No, it is better to double. Partner will picture this sort of hand and can make the best decision. Once again, you are sitting under the spade length, so your double is for take-out.

Finally, let's consider the situation where you have made a simple overcall on a hand that is quite strong for that action. Suppose you are sitting West and the auction unfolds like this:

West	West	North	East	South
♠ K J 10 7 6		Pass	Pass	1◇
♡ A K 4	1♠	2♣	Pass	Pass
◇ A 9 4	?			
♣ 7 2				

You have already shown five spades, so it would be inappropriate to rebid the suit. It is better to compete with a take-out double. If partner does hold some modicum of spade support, he can show it now. By doubling, you give partner the option of showing ♡J-x-x-x-x, or even of leaving in the double for penalties, should his hand contain something like ♣Q-10-9-x. Think of the second-round double as your 'flexible friend'!

Tip 27

Finesse in the no-loser suit

Sometimes you have no losers in a particular side suit but by conceding an unnecessary trick in the suit you can end-play one of the defenders. You like the sound of that? Here is an example of the play:

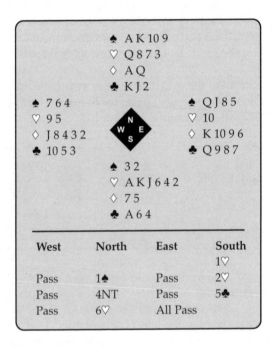

	♠ A K 10 9		
	♡ Q 8 7 3		
	◇ A Q		
	♣ K J 2		

♠ 7 6 4		♠ Q J 8 5
♡ 9 5		♡ 10
◇ J 8 4 3 2		◇ K 10 9 6
♣ 10 5 3		♣ Q 9 8 7

	♠ 3 2
	♡ A K J 6 4 2
	◇ 7 5
	♣ A 6 4

West	North	East	South
			1♡
Pass	1♠	Pass	2♡
Pass	4NT	Pass	5♣
Pass	6♡	All Pass	

How will you play the small slam in hearts when West leads the ♡5?

You have one potential loser in each of the minor suits and no losers in spades. Nevertheless it is in spades that you should take your finesse. You win the trump lead with the jack and cash the ace of trumps. Now you play a spade to the ten and jack. East has no safe return. You began with eleven top tricks and East's return, into one of dummy's three tenaces, will give you a twelfth trick.

The next deal is similar, except that you have to eliminate one of the three side suits before taking a finesse in the no-loser suit.

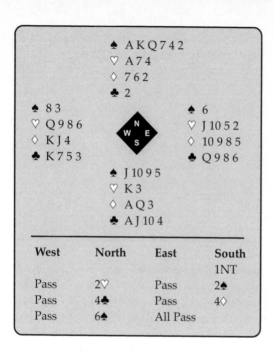

	♠ AKQ742		
	♡ A74		
	◊ 762		
	♣ 2		

West	North	East	South
			1NT
Pass	2♡	Pass	2♠
Pass	4♣	Pass	4◊
Pass	6♠	All Pass	

North began with a transfer response, showing at least five spades. A 3♣ rebid would have been natural and forcing to game. North's actual 4♣ was, in the system being played, a self-agreeing splinter bid. It showed a club shortage and suggested a slam in spades. How would you play the spade slam when West leads a trump?

After winning the trump lead, you should take the small risk of cashing the king and ace of hearts. You then ruff the third round of hearts with the ♠J, eliminating the suit. A trump to dummy will leave these cards still to be played:

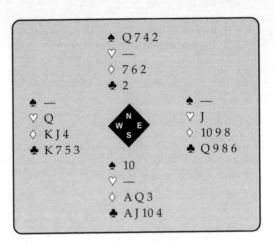

You finesse the ♣J, losing to the ♣K, and West has no good return. A heart will give a ruff-and-discard, allowing you to throw the ◊2 and ruff in the South hand. Dummy's other diamond loser will be thrown on the ♣A. A return of either minor by West will also give you the contract.

There's just enough space to accommodate one more example:

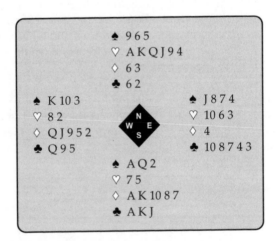

You play in 6♡ from the South seat after a transfer auction. You win the trump lead and draw trumps, throwing the ♠2 from your hand. If you try to establish the diamonds by ruffing, the 5-1 break will defeat you. Instead you should lead a diamond to the ten. West wins with the jack and is end-played. If he returns the ◊Q, you will win and ruff-finesse against his ◊9.

Tip
28

Kill dummy's
solid suit

S uppose declarer is playing in a suit contract and has a side suit with several top winners in the dummy. His intention will be to draw trumps and then to run the side suit. You can sometimes prevent this by playing a round or two of the side suit at an early stage. Your objective is to exhaust declarer of his cards in that suit, thereby preventing him from reaching the dummy after he has drawn trumps. Take the East cards here:

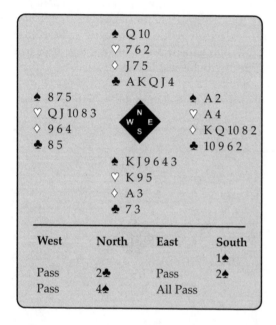

	♠ Q 10	
	♡ 7 6 2	
	◊ J 7 5	
	♣ A K Q J 4	
♠ 8 7 5		♠ A 2
♡ Q J 10 8 3		♡ A 4
◊ 9 6 4		◊ K Q 10 8 2
♣ 8 5		♣ 10 9 6 2
	♠ K J 9 6 4 3	
	♡ K 9 5	
	◊ A 3	
	♣ 7 3	

West	North	East	South
			1♠
Pass	2♣	Pass	2♠
Pass	4♠	All Pass	

West leads the ♡Q against the spade game. Sitting East, what is your plan for the defence?

How would many players defend with the East cards? Some would win with the ♡A and return a heart. It is not a promising line of defence. You can probably set up a heart winner for partner, yes, but it is unlikely that he will ever gain the lead to enjoy it. Declarer will force out the ace of trumps, win your return, draw trumps and run the clubs.

How about a switch to the ◇K, made in the hope that partner has only two diamonds and can be given a ruff. It's a possible defence, yes, but if South holds three diamonds he may have only one club and be able to take a quick discard.

The best idea is a switch to the ♣10. If West has only one club, you will be able to give him a club ruff. In the more likely case where the missing clubs are 2-2 between the West and South hands, you will be able to cut declarer off from dummy's long clubs. You switch to the ♣10, then, and West signals his doubleton with the ♣8. Declarer wins in the dummy and leads the ♣Q. What now?

If you capture this and play another club, declarer will play a third round of clubs, throwing a loser. West can ruff but when declarer regains the lead, he will cross to the ♠10, drawing the last two trumps, and enjoy the rest of the club suit. Instead, you must duck the first trump and win the second round. You return another club, cutting declarer's link with the dummy, and the contract is defeated. If declarer tries to cash a further club, West will ruff with his last trump.

Let's see another deal on this theme. Take the East cards here:

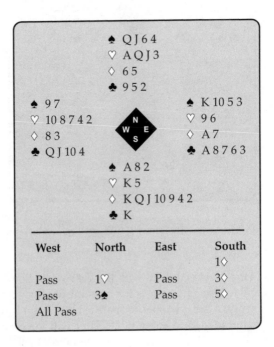

	♠ Q J 6 4		
	♡ A Q J 3		
	◇ 6 5		
	♣ 9 5 2		
♠ 9 7			♠ K 10 5 3
♡ 10 8 7 4 2			♡ 9 6
◇ 8 3			◇ A 7
♣ Q J 10 4			♣ A 8 7 6 3
	♠ A 8 2		
	♡ K 5		
	◇ K Q J 10 9 4 2		
	♣ K		

West	North	East	South
			1◇
Pass	1♡	Pass	3◇
Pass	3♠	Pass	5◇
All Pass			

West leads the ♣Q against the diamond game and you win with the ♣A, the ♣K dropping from South. How will you continue the defence?

South will not have attributed much value to the singleton ♣K, so you can place him with both the ♠A and the ♡K. To beat the diamond game, you will need to score your two minor-suit aces and a spade trick. Unfortunately, though, there is every possibility that declarer will be able to discard any potential spade loser on the surplus heart winners in dummy. What can you do about it?

The answer is that you should return a heart at trick two, aiming to cut declarer's link with the dummy. South wins with the ♡K and West plays the ♡2, showing you an odd number of cards in the suit. When declarer plays the ◊K, you win immediately with the ◊A and return a second round of hearts, putting declarer in the dummy for the last time.

The contract is doomed. If declarer tries to cash another round of hearts, you will ruff. Declarer can overruff but he cannot deprive you of your spade trick. If instead declarer leads the ♠Q from dummy, you will refuse to cover. Declarer will then have no option but to try another top heart and you will kill the contract by ruffing.

Tip
29

Lead towards
a doubleton honour

In this Tip we will look at some situations where you hold four or more cards opposite a doubleton honour. It is a blind spot among some players that the best chance of developing tricks may be to lead low towards the doubleton holding. Here is a straightforward example:

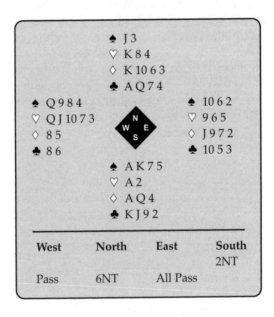

	♠ J 3	
	♡ K 8 4	
	♢ K 10 6 3	
	♣ A Q 7 4	
♠ Q 9 8 4		♠ 10 6 2
♡ Q J 10 7 3		♡ 9 6 5
♢ 8 5		♢ J 9 7 2
♣ 8 6		♣ 10 5 3
	♠ A K 7 5	
	♡ A 2	
	♢ A Q 4	
	♣ K J 9 2	

West	North	East	South
			2NT
Pass	6NT	All Pass	

West leads the ♡Q against your small slam. You have eleven tricks on top and the diamond suit offers an excellent chance of providing a twelfth trick. How will you play the contract?

There is no need to rely exclusively on a favourable diamond position. Win the heart lead with the ace and lead a low spade towards dummy's jack. When West holds the ♠Q, you will make a third spade trick and can claim twelve tricks before you even look at the diamond position.

There is another possible benefit from playing on spades. Suppose East's hand is ♠Q-10-6-2 ♡9-6-5, ♢J-9-7-2 ♣10-5. He wins the ♠J with the ♠Q, much to your disappointment, but you will still make the contract on any return. When you cash your winners in hearts and clubs, East will have to throw a spade or a diamond. Your twelfth trick will come from the suit that he discards.

A similar play is available on this deal:

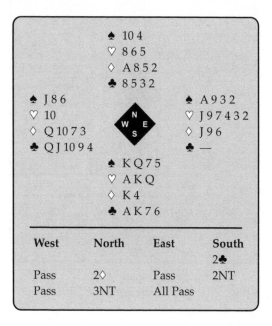

	♠ 10 4		
	♡ 8 6 5		
	◊ A 8 5 2		
	♣ 8 5 3 2		

♠ J 8 6		♠ A 9 3 2
♡ 10		♡ J 9 7 4 3 2
◊ Q 10 7 3		◊ J 9 6
♣ Q J 10 9 4		♣ —

	♠ K Q 7 5		
	♡ A K Q		
	◊ K 4		
	♣ A K 7 6		

West	North	East	South
			2♣
Pass	2◊	Pass	2NT
Pass	3NT	All Pass	

West leads the ♣Q against 3NT and East discards the ♡2. How will you play the contract?

You can count seven top tricks. If you can develop two spade tricks, this will bring your total to nine. The best play, after winning the club lead, is to lead a low spade towards the ten. When West holds the ♠J, as in the diagram, you are assured of two spade tricks, whether he rises with the ♠J or not.

The alternative line, with this spade holding, is to lead twice towards the ♠K-Q. It is not practical on this particular deal because you have only one entry to dummy.

We will end with a straightforward combination that is often misplayed. Test yourself in 3NT here:

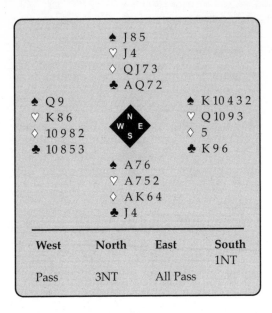

♠ J 8 5
♡ J 4
◇ Q J 7 3
♣ A Q 7 2

♠ Q 9
♡ K 8 6
◇ 10 9 8 2
♣ 10 8 5 3

♠ K 10 4 3 2
♡ Q 10 9 3
◇ 5
♣ K 9 6

♠ A 7 6
♡ A 7 5 2
◇ A K 6 4
♣ J 4

West	North	East	South
			1NT
Pass	3NT	All Pass	

How will you play 3NT when West leads the ◇10?

You have seven tricks on top and the only realistic chance of adding two more tricks lies in the club suit. Suppose you win the diamond lead in your hand and lead the ♣J. You will hardly ever score the three club tricks you need! If West holds the ♣K, he will cover and you will make just two tricks with the ace and queen.

A better idea is to follow this Tip and to lead towards the doubleton honour. You win the diamond lead in the dummy and lead a low club towards your ♣J-4. What can East do? If he rises with the ♣K, you will have the three club tricks that you need. Suppose instead that he plays low. Your ♣J will win and you can then duck a second round of clubs. When you subsequently cash the ♣A, East's ♣K will fall and dummy's ♣Q will be your ninth trick.

Tip
30
Save space with Kickback Blackwood

In tournament bridge it is universally popular to use Roman Key-card Blackwood (where the responses involve the four aces and the trump king and queen) instead of simple Blackwood. If you are unfamiliar with this convention, these are the main responses:

After a start of, say, 1♠ – 4NT, the opener will rebid:

5♣ – 0 or 3 of the five 'aces' (where the trump king counts as an 'ace')
5◊ – 1 or 4 of the five 'aces'
5♡ – 2 or 5 of the five 'aces' without the queen of trumps
5♠ – 2 or 5 of the five 'aces' with the queen of trumps

(Note that some players, particularly in the USA, swap the meanings given above for 5♣ and 5◊. The mnemonic for this alternative method is '1430 responses', because the first step shows 1 or 4 key cards and the second step shows 3 or 0 key cards.)

When partner responds 5♣ or 5◊, you can ask whether he holds the trump queen by making the next available bid that is not in the agreed trump suit. So, after a start of 1♠ – 4NT – 5♣ – 5◊, asking for the trump queen, the opener will rebid:

5♠ – 'I am signing off because I do not hold the trump queen'
5♡ – 'I have the trump queen and the ♡K'
5NT – 'I have the trump queen but no side-suit king'
6♣ – 'I have the trump queen and the ♣K'
6◊ – 'I have the trump queen and the ◊K'

When you hold the trump queen and two side-suit kings, you show the lower king first, perhaps showing the other king if there is space on the next round.

When the 4NT bidder continues on the next round with 5NT, he is telling you that all the key cards are present and asking you to cue-bid any side-suit king.

So much for Roman Key-card Blackwood. Perhaps you are already

---

familiar with the method and are muttering 'Call that a bridge tip?' to yourself! One of the problems with any form of Blackwood 4NT is that an unfavourable response can carry you too high (beyond five of the trump suit), when two big cards are missing. This is particularly so when the agreed suit is a minor. Look at this auction:

♠ Q 10 8		♠ K J	West	East
♡ K Q 6	N	♡ 7	1♣	1◇
◇ 5	W E	◇ A K Q 9 3	2♣	4NT
♣ A J 9 8 7 2	S	♣ K Q 10 5 4	5◇	...

It may seem a good idea to bid RKCB on the East hand, with clubs agreed, but the 'one key card' response carries you past the safety level of 5♣. You can try passing 5◇, hoping that partner will hold ◇x-x-x or ◇J-x for you. Not today!

The idea of Kickback Blackwood is to use a lower bid than 4NT to ask for key cards. This is the scheme:

> When clubs are agreed, 4◇ asks for key cards
> When diamonds are agreed, 4♡ asks for key cards
> When hearts are agreed, 4♠ asks for key cards
> When spades are agreed, 4NT asks for key cards.

So, the bid immediately beyond four of the agreed trump suit is used as Roman Key-card Blackwood. This does imply that this bid cannot be used as a cue-bid, which it would have been if you were using 4NT as the Blackwood bid. You can compensate to some extent by using 4NT to show a cue-bid in the suit that is no longer available in the normal way.

Let's bid the previous hand, using Kickback Blackwood:

♠ Q 10 8		♠ K J	West	East
♡ K Q 6	N	♡ 7	1♣	1◇
◇ 5	W E	◇ A K Q 9 3	2♣	4◇
♣ A J 9 8 7 2	S	♣ K Q 10 5 4	4♠	5♣

East's 4◇, one bid beyond four of the agreed trump suit (clubs) is Kickback Blackwood. West's second-step response of 4♠ shows 1 or 4 key cards and East is then able to sign off at a safe level.

Another 52 Great Bridge Tips

Some players (very few experts, though) reserve a bid of 4♣ to ask for aces, whether the contract will be in no-trumps or a suit. This convention, known as Gerber, is popular in some quarters. The reason why experts are so snooty about players who use Gerber in suit auctions is that it is normally employed to the exclusion of control-showing cue bids. Since cue bids allow you to suggest a slam without going past the game level, also to check up that every side suit is controlled, they are rightly regarded as indispensable in slam bidding. Look at this start to the auction:

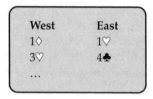

West	East
1◇	1♡
3♡	4♣
...	

East's bid of 4♣ is a control-showing cue bid. It passes these messages:

(a) I have the ace (or king, for some players) of clubs
(b) I do not have the ace (or king) of spades
(c) I have the extra strength to visualise a possible slam

West now has the option to sign off, to make a further cue bid or to bid Blackwood. You can see how valuable such a cue bid is. Those who treat 4♣ as Gerber in this type of auction lose a huge amount. They can bid 4♣ only on the rare occasions when all they need to know is the number of aces that partner holds.

When you play Kickback, you do not lose the ability to cue bid. Remember that 4NT replaces the only cue bid that has been lost because it is now being used to ask for key cards.

Let's finish the Tip with a couple of auctions that use Kickback Blackwood to good effect.

			West	East
♠ 5		♠ A K 6	1♣	1◇
♡ A Q 3	N W E S	♡ 7 6	3◇	4♡
◇ K Q 7 5		◇ A 10 8 6 2	4♠	4NT
♣ A J 9 8 2		♣ K Q 4	5NT	7◇

East's 4♡ (one level beyond four of the agreed diamond suit) is Kickback Blackwood. The first-step response of 4♠ shows 0 or 3 key cards, clearly three after West's strong rebid. The next available bid, not in the trump suit, is 4NT. This bid therefore asks for the trump queen. West's 5NT says 'I do have the trump queen but no side-suit king.' East now bids the grand slam, hoping to score five diamonds, five clubs, the ace of hearts and the ace-king of spades. If West's clubs are only A-9-x-x-x and need to be ruffed good because of a 4-1 break, then a spade ruff may provide the thirteenth trick instead.

♠ Q J 3		♠ A	West	East
♡ J 9 7 2	**N**	♡ A K Q 6 5 4	1NT	3♡
◇ K J 7	**W** **E**	◇ A Q 2	4♣	4♠
♣ A 10 4	**S**	♣ K Q 7	5♣	5♠
			6◇	7NT

East's 3♡ shows a six-card suit (he would use a 2◇ transfer bid with only five hearts) and West's 4♣ is a cue bid, showing a heart fit and the ♣A. East bids 4♠ (Kickback) and hears of one key card, which must be the ♣A. If he needed to ask about the queen of trumps, East would continue with 5◇, the next available non-trump bid. His actual 5♠, the next available bid not in the trump suit, asks partner to name any side-suit king. West's 6◇ proclaims the ◇K and East can then bid the grand slam in notrumps.

As you can imagine, it may take a while to get familiar with using different bids to ask for key-cards. It is the same with the follow-up bids, to enquire about the trump queen and side-suit kings. Is it worth all the effort? You must decide!

Another 52 Great Bridge Tips

Tip

31

Endplay the defender who becomes trump-heavy

When you are defending, you are normally very happy to have a strong trump holding. Not always! Sometimes your trumps may become an embarrassment in the end position. You will be forced to ruff and then give away a trick. In this Tip we will look at such positions from declarer's point of view. Take the South cards on this deal:

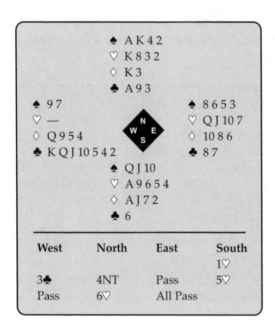

♠ A K 4 2
♡ K 8 3 2
◇ K 3
♣ A 9 3

♠ 9 7
♡ —
◇ Q 9 5 4
♣ K Q J 10 5 4 2

♠ 8 6 5 3
♡ Q J 10 7
◇ 10 8 6
♣ 8 7

♠ Q J 10
♡ A 9 6 5 4
◇ A J 7 2
♣ 6

West	North	East	South
			1♡
3♣	4NT	Pass	5♡
Pass	6♡	All Pass	

North, who has a high regard for your cardplay, carries you to a small slam. How will you play the contract when West leads the ♣K?

The hands fit together very well and the only possible problem is a 4-0 trump break. What can you do about it? If anyone holds four trumps, it is likely to be East, who holds five clubs fewer than his partner. So, you should lead a low trump from the North hand, intending to cover with the ♡9 if East produces the ♡7. You will not mind at all if West wins the trick because this will mean that the trumps are breaking 3-1 at worst.

If East does play the ♡7 on the first round, a finesse of the ♡9 will win.

You can then cash the king and ace of trumps, discard one diamond loser on the spades and ruff the other. A more interesting situation will arise if East senses your intended safety play and prevents it by playing the ♡10 on the first round. What then?

You win with the ♡A and must now try to restrict East to just one trump trick, even though he holds ♡Q-J-7 sitting over dummy's ♡K-9-3. How can this be done? You must aim for a three-card ending where East has nothing left but his trumps. You can then catch East in an end-play. How does the play go?

You need East to hold at least three spades, so this is the suit that you play first. When West shows out on the third round of spades, you continue with a fourth round, discarding a diamond. You ruff a club in your hand, cash the ◇K and ◇A and ruff a diamond in dummy. These cards remain:

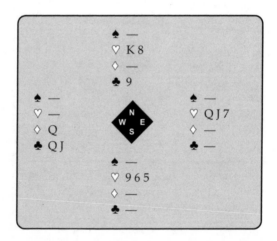

When you lead the ♣9 from the North hand, East has to ruff with an honour to prevent you scoring the ♡9 in your hand. He then has to lead away from his remaining trump honour into dummy's ♡K-8 tenace. The last two tricks are yours!

Here is another example of this style of play:

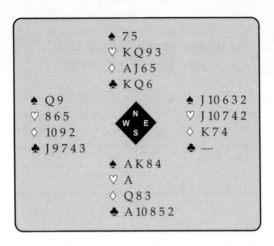

West leads the ◊10 against your small slam in clubs and you rise with dummy's ◊A. You cross to the ♡A and return to dummy with the ♣K, alarmed to see East discard a heart. How will you continue?

You discard your diamond losers on the ♡K-Q and ruff a diamond in your hand. You then cash the ♠A-K and lead another spade. West discards a diamond and you ruff with the ♣6. These cards remain:

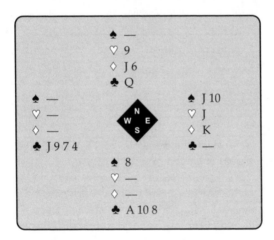

You cash dummy's ♣Q and play a heart or a diamond, discarding your ♠8. The trump-heavy West has to ruff partner's winner and lead a trump into your ♣A-10 tenace. Twelve tricks good and true.

Tip 32

Play 'third hand low' to kill an entry

Ⅰn this Tip we will see some deals where playing 'third hand high' is a mistake because it gives an extra entry to dummy. You are East here:

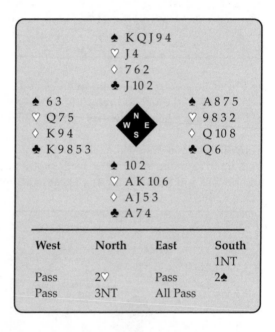

	North	East	South
West			1NT
Pass	2♡	Pass	2♠
Pass	3NT	All Pass	

Your partner, West, leads the ♣5 against 3NT. What is your plan for the defence when the ♣J is played from dummy?

At least half of the world's Easts (maybe I'm being ungenerous!) will play the ♣Q. Declarer wins and plays on spades. Even if East holds up the ♠A, declarer will eventually reach dummy with the ♣10 to enjoy the long cards. The same would happen if South held ♣K-7-4 instead.

Sitting East, you should play low at trick one, aiming to kill the club entry to dummy. Declarer plays on spades and you win the second round. You return the ♣Q and clubs are cleared. The contract cannot then be made.

Rising with the ♣Q is a good idea only when West holds the ♣A-K, which is very unlikely on this bidding. It would mean that South had no stopper in either black suit for his strong 1NT opening. Playing low, the recommended play, stands a great chance of killing dummy's spade suit.

On the next deal you can tell the right play by counting declarer's points.

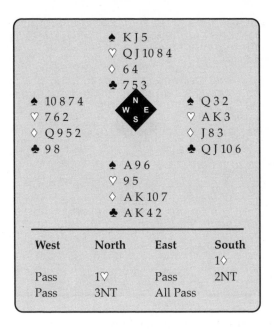

West	North	East	South
			1♦
Pass	1♡	Pass	2NT
Pass	3NT	All Pass	

West leads the ♠4 against 3NT and the ♠5 is played from dummy. Sitting East, what is your plan for the defence?

Most of the world's East players (there I go again) would play their ♣Q. Declarer would win with the ♠A and lead the ♡9. With two spade entries available to the dummy it would then make no difference whether East holds up in hearts. Declarer would score three spades, three hearts and the two ace-kings in the minors, ending with an overtrick.

Let's go back to trick one. South's 2NT jump rebid showed 18-19 points, so East knows that he holds the ♠A. There is no point whatsoever in expending the ♠Q at trick one. By doing so, East gives the dummy a second entry in the spade suit. Suppose East plays low on the first trick. If declarer wins with the ♠9 and leads the ♡9, West will give a count signal to show three hearts and East will allow the ♡9 to win. Declarer will then make only one heart trick and the contract will go one down.

(A skilled declarer would, in fact, win the first trick with the ♠A, rather than the ♠9. This would give him the necessary two entries to dummy if West held the ♠Q and a subsequent finesse of the ♠J succeeded.)

We will end the Tip with a more difficult deal, where declarer needs an entry to dummy in order to take a finesse. Take the East cards here:

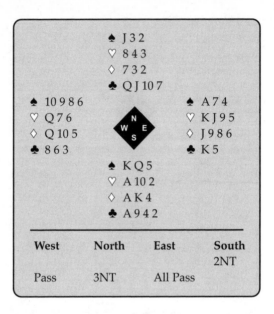

```
                        ♠ J 3 2
                        ♡ 8 4 3
                        ◇ 7 3 2
                        ♣ Q J 10 7
     ♠ 10 9 8 6                          ♠ A 7 4
     ♡ Q 7 6              N              ♡ K J 9 5
     ◇ Q 10 5          W     E          ◇ J 9 8 6
     ♣ 8 6 3              S              ♣ K 5
                        ♠ K Q 5
                        ♡ A 10 2
                        ◇ A K 4
                        ♣ A 9 4 2
```

West	North	East	South
			2NT
Pass	3NT	All Pass	

West leads the ♠10, dummy playing low. How will you defend?

Most defenders would win with the ♠A and then sit back in their chair wondering what to do next. Too late! Declarer will unblock the ♠Q (or ♠K) under the ♠A. When he gains the lead at some stage he will be able to cross to the ♠J to take the club finesse. This will give him four club tricks for a total of nine.

To beat the game, you must play low at trick one. Your partner cannot hold ♠K-Q-10-9(-x), after South's 2NT opening. Nor would he have led the ♠10 even if he did have that combination. So, South must hold at least the ♠K or the ♠Q, probably both. He is certain to make at least one trick from the suit anyway and it cannot cost you to hold up the ♠A on the first round. By doing so, you will kill declarer's entry to the dummy. Unable to take a club finesse, he will go one down.

**Count the hand
to diagnose
a deep finesse**

'Well, you could make it by taking a deep finesse in clubs, but that would be double-dummy.' Many a post mortem concludes in this fashion. On some deals, however, you can obtain a complete count on the defenders' hands and a deep finesse then becomes a sure-fire prospect. Here is a typical example:

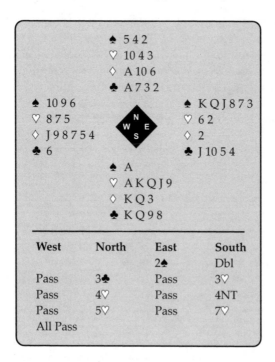

	♠ 542		
	♡ 1043		
	◊ A106		
	♣ A732		

♠ 1096   ♠ KQJ873
♡ 875   ♡ 62
◊ J98754   ◊ 2
♣ 6   ♣ J1054

	♠ A		
	♡ AKQJ9		
	◊ KQ3		
	♣ KQ98		

West	North	East	South
		2♠	Dbl
Pass	3♣	Pass	3♡
Pass	4♡	Pass	4NT
Pass	5♡	Pass	7♡
All Pass			

North-South are playing Lebensohl responses to the double of a weak two-bid (see Tip 42). North's 3♣ therefore shows 8-10 points and South's change of suit is forcing. How would you play the grand slam when West leads the ten of spades?

You win and draw trumps in three rounds, East following twice. To make the slam you must now pick up the clubs. All will be easy if the suit breaks 3-2. What if clubs are 4-1?

If East holds a singleton ♣J or ♣10 it would fall when you cashed the king. You could then continue with the ♣Q and run the ♣9 on the third round to pick up West's initial ♣10-x-x-x or ♣J-x-x-x. Suppose you cashed the ♣K and West produced an honour. You would then cross to the ♣A and pick up an initial ♣10-x-x-x or ♣J-x-x-x with East.

Rather than guess what to do, you should make the cost-nothing play of cashing the king and queen of diamonds. Here East will show out on the second round, which marks him with 6-2-1-4 shape. Since East holds four clubs, you should play a club to the ace on the first round. You continue with a low club, intending to finesse the nine. If East splits his ♣J-10, you win and return to the diamond ace for a club finesse.

Suppose instead that East had followed to two rounds of diamonds. It would then be impossible for him to hold four clubs. You would cash the ♣K on the first round, hoping that if East held only one club it would be the jack or ten. As discussed above, you could then continue with the ♣Q and run the ♣9 on the third round, again making the contract.

Now that you have the idea, test yourself on this deal:

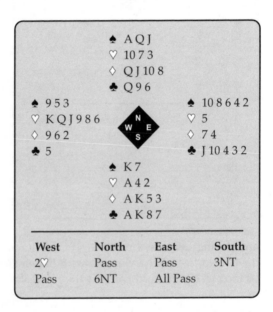

	♠ A Q J		
	♡ 10 7 3		
	◇ Q J 10 8		
	♣ Q 9 6		

♠ 9 5 3			♠ 10 8 6 4 2
♡ K Q J 9 8 6			♡ 5
◇ 9 6 2			◇ 7 4
♣ 5			♣ J 10 4 3 2

	♠ K 7		
	♡ A 4 2		
	◇ A K 5 3		
	♣ A K 8 7		

West	North	East	South
2♡	Pass	Pass	3NT
Pass	6NT	All Pass	

West leads the ♡K, which you might as well duck. (This would lead to a simple squeeze on West, should he hold four clubs alongside his heart suit.) West continues with a second round of hearts, East throwing a spade, and you win with the ace. What now?

All depends on bringing in the clubs. In case a guess develops in that suit, you should seek a complete count on the hand. You begin with the ace, king and queen of diamonds, West showing up with three cards in the suit and East discarding another spade. When you continue with three rounds of spades, both defenders follow all the way. The shape of the West hand is now known to be 3-6-3-1. You cash the ♣Q to take a look at West's singleton club. He produces the ♣5.

You must be careful now not to block the club suit. You lead the ♣9, intending to run the card. It will not help East to cover with the ♣J or ♣10 because you will win in the South hand and return to dummy with the ◊J to finesse the ♣8 on the next round.

Here is a final example. Once again, it features an opposing pre-empt, which is a good reminder of how such bids greatly assist you in building up a picture of the defenders' distributions.

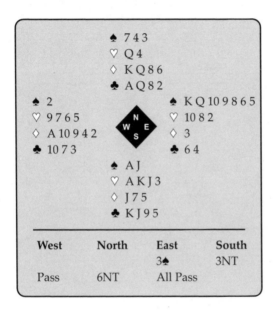

	♠ 7 4 3		
	♡ Q 4		
	◊ K Q 8 6		
	♣ A Q 8 2		

♠ 2   ♠ K Q 10 9 8 6 5
♡ 9 7 6 5   ♡ 10 8 2
◊ A 10 9 4 2   ◊ 3
♣ 10 7 3   ♣ 6 4

♠ A J
♡ A K J 3
◊ J 7 5
♣ K J 9 5

West	North	East	South
		3♠	3NT
Pass	6NT	All Pass	

Cast aside any doubts you may have about the bidding. How will you play 6NT when West leads the ♠2?

It's not a brilliant contract, of course, but the spade suit appears to be breaking 7-1. If West holds the ◊A, you are in with a chance. How many top tricks do you have? One spade, four hearts and four clubs, for a total of nine. You therefore need three diamond tricks for the slam. All will be well if the suit breaks 3-3. Failing that, you may need to finesse the ◊8 at some stage. Before committing yourself in diamonds, you should test the other side suits.

You win the spade lead and cash four rounds of hearts, throwing two spades from dummy. You note with interest that East follows three times. When you continue with the ace and queen of clubs, East follows both times. East cannot hold more than one diamond now. You lead a low diamond from dummy to your jack, East producing the ◊3 and West winning with the ◊A.

Let's assume that West is a cunning character and produces a cool ◊4 next. You will take a deep finesse of dummy's ◊8! You know from your count of the hand that this play will be successful. If instead West exits with a club, you will win with the jack and lead a diamond, intending to finesse the ◊8. It will do West no good to split his ◊10-9 because you have a further club entry to your hand to lead a third round of diamonds.

Tip 34

Rebid 1NT with a singleton in partner's suit

When your 1NT opening shows 12-14 points, a 1NT rebid should show 15-17 points. If instead you prefer a strong 1NT of 15-17 points, a 1NT rebid will indicate 12-14 points. In both cases you should be willing to rebid 1NT when you hold a singleton in partner's suit.

Let's suppose first that you are playing a 12-14 point 1NT and hold one of these hands:

(1)	(2)	(3)
♠ 4	♠ A Q 3	♠ 8
♡ A Q 5 4	♡ 4	♡ 10 9 7 4
◇ Q 10 7 5	◇ K J 8 6	◇ A Q 8 5
♣ A K 8 4	♣ A Q 9 7 3	♣ A Q J 3

On hand (1) you open 1♣ (better than 1◇ when you are 4-4 in the minors, since you allow a fit to be found immediately in either minor). If partner responds 1♠, you should rebid 1NT, showing 15-17 points. When partner is weak, this is likely to be your best contract. How else are you going to get there if you are not willing to rebid 1NT with a singleton?

With hand (2) you again open 1♣. If partner responds 1♡, you are somewhat light for a reverse into 2◇. Instead you should rebid 1NT, giving a good picture of your overall strength. Once more, this is likely to be the best contract when partner is weak. With the minor suits the other way round, you would probably choose to open 1◇ and rebid 2♣, giving a clearer picture of the hand.

On hand (3) you cannot rebid 1NT since you do not hold 15-17 points. You will find some wild characters who open a weak 1NT despite holding a singleton. (This is not recommended, except perhaps when your singleton is an honour. In any case, it would have to be declared on your convention card). So that you will have a rebid after a 1♠ response, you should open 1◇, planning to rebid 2♣.

Now let's say you are playing a strong 1NT of 15-17 points. How will you bid the same three hands:

(1)	(2)	(3)
♠ 4	♠ A Q 3	♠ 8
♡ A Q 5 4	♡ 4	♡ 10 9 7 4
◇ Q 10 7 5	◇ K J 8 6	◇ A Q 8 5
♣ A K 8 4	♣ A Q 9 7 3	♣ A Q J 3

As we noted before, some players are willing to open 1NT on hand (1). Go ahead with this if you want, but don't blame me if you occasionally get a bad result. The orthodox way to bid the hand is to open 1◇, intending to rebid 2♣ over 1♠ (because a 1NT rebid would be weak).

Hand (2) is a bit of a problem. You are around a point light for a reverse sequence (1♣ – 1♡ – 2◇). The old-timers' solution, opening 1◇ and rebidding 2♣ over 1♡, has fallen out of favour because you often end in a 4-2 diamond fit. It is probably best to overstate your strength slightly, making a reverse on the hand.

Hand (3) gives you no problem. You can open 1♣, or 1◇ if that is your preference, intending to rebid 1NT (weak) after a response of 1♠.

These is a typical situation where the Tip will perform well:

		West	East
♠ 8	♠ K J 7 3 2	1◇	1♠
♡ 10 9 7 4	♡ Q 8 3	1NT	
◇ A Q 8 5	◇ 10 6		
♣ A Q J 3	♣ 9 7 4		

You may make 1NT, you may not. In any case, it is a much better contract than the one that would result from the traditional sequence on these hands: 1◇ – 1♠ – 2♣ – 2◇.

Tip

35

**Test one suit
to determine
your line of play**

I t sometimes happens that you cannot tell which line of play will be best until you have tested one of the suits. Let's see an example of this:

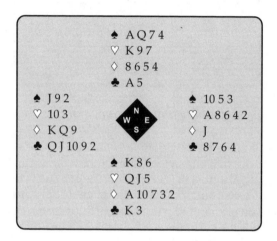

♠ A Q 7 4
♡ K 9 7
◊ 8 6 5 4
♣ A 5

♠ J 9 2
♡ 10 3
◊ K Q 9
♣ Q J 10 9 2

♠ 10 5 3
♡ A 8 6 4 2
◊ J
♣ 8 7 6 4

♠ K 8 6
♡ Q J 5
◊ A 10 7 3 2
♣ K 3

How will you play 3NT when West leads the ♣Q?

You have six tricks on top, possibly seven if the spades break 3-3. Where should you seek your extra tricks, in hearts or in diamonds? The answer is that you cannot tell until you know how the spades are breaking. You win the club lead in either hand and play three rounds of spades. When they divide 3-3, you have seven tricks on top and will clearly play on hearts next, establishing for certain the two extra tricks that you need.

Suppose the spades had divided 4-2 or worse. With only six tricks on top you would need to play on diamonds, hoping for a 2-2 break there. If you played ace and another diamond on the present lay-out, of course, you would not make the contract. West would win the second round of diamonds and clear the club suit. You would then go two down.

A similar situation arises when you have a potential safety play in one suit. Whether or not you can afford to take it may depend on whether there is a loser in a different suit. In that case you must test the other suit first. See what you make of this deal:

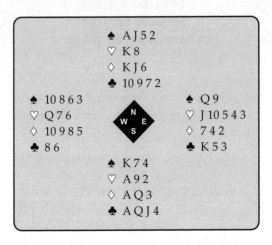

♠ A J 5 2
♡ K 8
◇ K J 6
♣ 10 9 7 2

♠ 10 8 6 3
♡ Q 7 6
◇ 10 9 8 5
♣ 8 6

♠ Q 9
♡ J 10 5 4 3
◇ 7 4 2
♣ K 5 3

♠ K 7 4
♡ A 9 2
◇ A Q 3
♣ A Q J 4

How will you play 6NT when West leads the ◇10?

The spade suit offers a safety play in a situation where you need only three spade tricks, rather than four. You can cash the ace and king on the first two rounds, planning to lead towards the jack on the third round. In this way you score your required three spade tricks when East began with a doubleton queen. (You will also score three spade tricks, of course, when West holds the ♠Q or the suit breaks 3-3.) If instead you need a full four spade tricks, you must play the suit differently. You must finesse the ♠J in the hope that West began with ♠Q-x-x.

Can you afford the safety play for three spade tricks or not? You have eight tricks outside the spade suit if the ♣K is with West, nine tricks if it is with East. So, you must test the lie of the club suit before you can tell how to play the spades. You win the diamond lead in the dummy and run the ♣10. When this wins the trick you continue with a club to the jack. You now know that you have four club tricks and can therefore give yourself the maximum chance of scoring the three spade tricks that you need to make the slam. You continue with the ace and king of spades, intending to lead towards the spade jack on the third round. The ♠Q falls on the second round, as it happens, and you make the slam.

Suppose West had turned up with the ♣K. Needing a full four spade tricks, you would have cashed the ♠K and finessed the ♠J, hoping to find West with ♠Q-x-x.

Tip 36

Play the queen from A-Q-x to force declarer's king

There are some types of play that you might miss for a lifetime if they were never brought to your attention. The correct defence on the East hand below falls into this category.

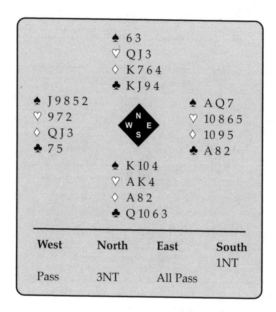

	♠ 6 3		
	♡ Q J 3		
	◊ K 7 6 4		
	♣ K J 9 4		
♠ J 9 8 5 2			♠ A Q 7
♡ 9 7 2			♡ 10 8 6 5
◊ Q J 3			◊ 10 9 5
♣ 7 5			♣ A 8 2
	♠ K 10 4		
	♡ A K 4		
	◊ A 8 2		
	♣ Q 10 6 3		

West	North	East	South
			1NT
Pass	3NT	All Pass	

You are sitting East and West leads the ♠5 against 3NT. What is your plan for the defence?

Suppose first that you 'do what comes naturally' and win with the ♠A. When you return the ♠Q declarer will hold up the ♠K, aiming to break the communications between the defenders. He wins the third round of spades, crosses his fingers and plays on clubs. On this occasion the finger manoeuvre will pay dividends. The ♣A will turn up in the safe East hand and the contract will be made.

Now use a bit of imagination and try the effect of playing the ♠Q at trick one. If your partner has led from something like ♠K-9-8-5-2, nothing will be lost. You can continue with ace and another spade. What will happen when the cards lie as in the diagram, though? Declarer can hardly risk holding up the ♠K because he might then lose four spades and a club, going down even when spades were 4-4 and the lead was from ♠A-J-9-5. So, South is likely to win the first round of spades and knock out the ♣A. You will continue with ace and another spade, allowing your partner to score his long cards in the suit for one down.

The time to make this deceptive play is when you hold a high card in a suit that you expect declarer to develop. (Here you held the ♣A.) Since you are the defender who will probably gain the lead, it is important to force out declarer's stopper in the suit led, to preserve communications with your partner.

Suppose instead that your partner holds the defensive stopper:

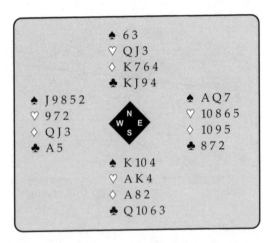

Again he leads the ♠5 against 3NT. It would be a poor idea to play the ♠Q now. Declarer would win with the ♠K and knock out the ♣A. Not expecting you to hold the ♠A, West might think that a switch to the ◊Q was the best chance for the defence! Instead, you should win the first trick with the ♠A and continue with the ♠Q, making life easy for partner.

Tip 37

Drop the honour in the danger hand

When one of the defenders has become a 'danger hand' (he holds some cashable winners, or can lead through a king in your hand), you must do everything you can to prevent him from gaining the lead. In particular, when you are developing a suit of your own you may need to play it in an unusual way. Let's begin with a straightforward example:

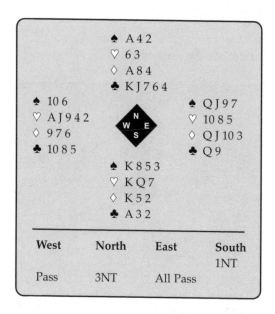

West leads the ♡4 against 3NT, East playing the ♡10. How will you play the contract?

A hold-up (allowing the ♡10 to win) would break communication between the defenders only when hearts were 6-2. This is not possible here because West led a fourth-best four of hearts and there is only one lower spot-card missing. West cannot hold more than five hearts and you should therefore win the first trick, with the heart queen. What next?

You have seven top tricks and will need to establish the club suit. The 'normal play' when you are missing five cards to the queen is to cash the

♣A and then finesse the ♣J. If you follow that line here, East (the danger hand) will win with the ♣Q. A heart return, through your K-7, will then spell defeat. Since you need only four club tricks for the contract, you should play the king and ace of clubs first. When the cards lie as in the diagram, the queen will fall doubleton and you will score an overtrick. Suppose the queen does not fall. You will still make the contract when West holds the ♣Q! You lead towards the ♣J on the third round and score the four club tricks that you need.

By playing the club suit in this way, you make the contract in two situations: when West holds the ♣Q and when East holds a doubleton (or singleton) ♣Q. Note that if West plays the ♣Q on the first round, when you lead towards dummy's ♣K, you should allow this card to win. By doing so, you would prevent East from gaining the lead when he held ♣10-9-8-5.

Here is another deal on the same theme:

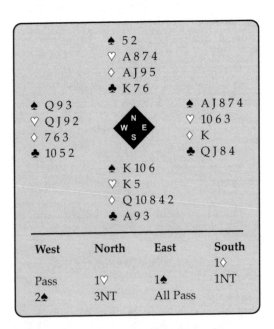

	♠ 5 2	
	♡ A 8 7 4	
	◊ A J 9 5	
	♣ K 7 6	
♠ Q 9 3		♠ A J 8 7 4
♡ Q J 9 2		♡ 10 6 3
◊ 7 6 3		◊ K
♣ 10 5 2		♣ Q J 8 4
	♠ K 10 6	
	♡ K 5	
	◊ Q 10 8 4 2	
	♣ A 9 3	

West	North	East	South
			1◊
Pass	1♡	1♠	1NT
2♣	3NT	All Pass	

West leads the ♠3 and East wins with the ♠A. How will you play the contract when East returns the ♠7 at trick two?

You should hold up the ♠K until the third round, aiming to break the defenders' communications when spades break 5-3 as the bidding indicates. What then?

You have six top tricks and will need to develop the diamond suit to cross the finishing line. If West holds the ◇K, all will be easy. A simple finesse would give you five diamond tricks and you would score an overtrick. Since you need only four diamond tricks for the contract, you can afford a safety play that aims to keep the danger hand off lead. You should play a diamond to the ace. When the cards lie as in the diagram, the singleton king falls from East and an overtrick is yours.

Suppose both defenders followed with a spot-card under the ◇A. Nothing would have been lost! You would continue to play diamonds and still make the contract when West held the diamond king. By following the recommended line you would make the contract in two situations: when West held the ◇K and when East held a singleton ◇K.

(Do you see how East might have defended more cleverly? Suppose he has read Tip 36 in this book and plays the ♠J at trick one, aiming to force out your stopper. Even if you sense the position and hold up the ♠K, East can continue with a low spade and you will have to win the second round. With the defenders' communications in spades intact, you will have little reason to spurn the diamond finesse and are likely to go down.)

Tip 38

Vary your pre-empts in the third seat

The bidding has started with two passes and, in the third seat, you find yourself staring at some moderate collection. What should you do? The general answer is: bid something! The opponents will find life much easier if they have the auction to themselves. You should therefore aim to obstruct them as often as is practical. One way to do this is to pre-empt at the three-level on some hands that would not justify such an action in the first or second seats.

Suppose the first two players pass and you hold one of these hands:

	(1)		(2)		(3)
♠	8 2	♠	5	♠	J 4
♡	10 4	♡	K 9 7 4	♡	—
◇	J 9 2	◇	K J 10 9 6 4 2	◇	Q J 8 3
♣	K Q J 10 7 2	♣	7	♣	J 9 8 6 5 4 2

Hand (1) contains only a six-card suit, but it fulfils admirably the general guidelines for a hand worthy of pre-emption: you will make a lot more tricks if you choose trumps than if you defend a contract by the opponents. Don't worry at all about opening 3♣ in the third seat. It is the obvious action! The hand is so suitable for a pre-empt that many players would open 3♣ in the first or second seat. In a Pairs event, there are many who would take the same action even when vulnerable.

Look next at hand (2). The text books may say that you should not pre-empt with a four-card major on the side, in case you miss a fit there. Suppose you are in the third seat, however, opposite a passed hand. So what if partner holds four or more hearts? In that case the opponents will have a massive fit in one of the black suits. So, go ahead and open 3◇. For similar reasons, many players (including me) would open 3◇ in the first or second seat too. Don't be one of those players who always find an excuse not to pre-empt.

On hand (3) the seven-card suit is very weak and you might not open 3♣ in the first or second seat. You should do so in the third seat, however.

You can just imagine the fourth player's hand. He probably holds upwards of 16 points with some great holdings in the majors. Make life difficult for him! Nearly everyone uses take-out doubles nowadays, so that there is virtually no risk of the defenders being able to double you for penalties. Note that this is not true when you open in the first seat (or even in the second seat), the bidding might then continue Pass – Pass – Dble and the player to your left could leave in the double for penalties.

It is also good tactics to open with a three-bid in the third seat when your hand is strong enough for a normal one-bid in a minor suit. By doing so, you leave your LHO with two choices: he must pass or enter at a high level, possibly risking a penalty double from your partner. Suppose the first two players pass and you hold one of these hands:

(4)	(5)	(6)
♠ 2	♠ J 9 7 2	♠ Q 4
♡ 10 4	♡ 4	♡ —
◇ A Q J 10 8 7 2	◇ A	◇ A J 10 9 8 3
♣ A 7 2	♣ K Q J 10 8 5 2	♣ K J 6 5 4

Open 3◇ on hand (4). Yes, you might miss a good 3NT once in a while. It is many times more likely that your LHO holds a sound hand with major-suit values and will be greatly inconvenienced by your bid.

Bid 3♣ on hand (5). When your LHO holds length in hearts, but not spades, he will be unable to double for take-out. You are leaving him with only two bids, 3♡ or 4♡. If his actual hearts are not that strong, he may not be willing to risk an overcall at the three-level. You may buy the contract in 3♣ when a 1♣ opening would have allowed the opponents to investigate their prospects in comfort.

Similarly, open 3◇ on hand (6). There is no point looking only on the black side ('I'm not opening 3◇ on that. We might miss a club game!'). There is always some risk attached to making a pre-empt. You must consider matters in the long term. On balance, a 3◇ opening is likely to prove a big thorn in your LHO's side.

Tip 39

Lead a low card on the first round

There are several suit holdings where you do best to lead a low card on the first round, rather than the top card. Test yourself on this deal:

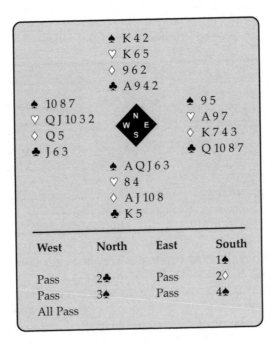

	♠ K 4 2	
	♡ K 6 5	
	♦ 9 6 2	
	♣ A 9 4 2	

♠ 10 8 7		♠ 9 5
♡ Q J 10 3 2	W E	♡ A 9 7
♦ Q 5	N S	♦ K 7 4 3
♣ J 6 3		♣ Q 10 8 7

	♠ A Q J 6 3	
	♡ 8 4	
	♦ A J 10 8	
	♣ K 5	

West	North	East	South
			1♠
Pass	2♣	Pass	2♦
Pass	3♠	Pass	4♠
All Pass			

West leads the ♡Q and the defenders persist with hearts, forcing you to ruff the third round. How will you continue?

You draw trumps in three rounds, ending in the dummy. You must now tackle the diamond suit. Which is the right card to lead from dummy? Time after time, you will see players leading the ♦9 in this situation. What will happen then? The nine loses to West's queen and a fourth round of hearts forces declarer to ruff with his last trump. He crosses to the ♣A and leads another diamond, finessing the jack. The finesse wins all right but the lead is then in the wrong hand. There is no way back to dummy and East's remaining ♦K-7 cannot be caught.

In this situation, and many similar positions, you do better to lead a low card on the first round. After drawing trumps, you should lead the ◊2 and play the ◊J from the South hand, losing to the ◊Q. You ruff the heart return, cross to dummy with the ♣A and (only then) lead the precious ◊9. East plays low and you can leave the lead in dummy by underplaying with your ◊8. The second finesse wins and you continue with the ◊6 to your ◊10, scoring the three diamond tricks that you need.

Here is another deal on the same theme, one where many declarers would go wrong.

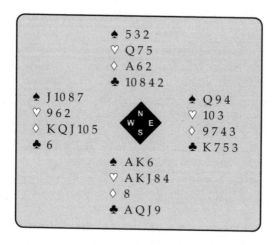

You arrive in 6♡ and West leads the ◊K. What is your plan?

Suppose you win with the ◊A and draw trumps, ending in the dummy. You lead the ♣10, which East refuses to cover, and you underplay with the ♣9. The finesse succeeds and the lead is left in dummy. You continue with a club to the queen and West shows out. There is no way back to dummy, so you will lose a club trick as well as a spade trick. One down!

Do you see how to do better? At trick two, after winning the diamond lead, you must lead a low club from dummy to your queen. You draw trumps, ending in the dummy, and (only then) lead the ♣10. When East refuses to cover, you underplay with the ♣9, leaving the lead in dummy. What a difference! You can now lead a low club on the third round, finessing the ♣J and making the slam.

There is another, quite different, reason for leading low on the first round of a suit – to avoid losing a trick when the defender in the second seat holds a singleton honour. Look at the diamond suit here:

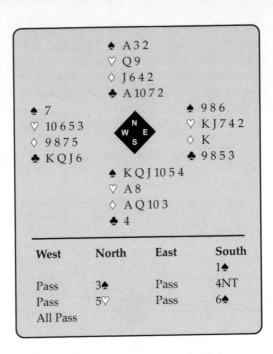

West	North	East	South
			1♠
Pass	3♠	Pass	4NT
Pass	5♡	Pass	6♠
All Pass			

The bidding is not from the top drawer, I agree, but how will you play the spade slam when West leads the ♣K?

Suppose you win with the ♣A and draw trumps in three rounds, ending in the dummy. In order to pick up a possible ◇K-x-x in the East hand, you will have to lead the ◇J next. East will cover with the bare ◇K and West's ◇9 will be promoted. You will lose a diamond as well as a heart.

In order to pick up a singleton ◇K onside, you must lead low on the first round. You cannot afford to do this after drawing trumps, or you would fail to pick up ◇K-x-x, so you must do it at trick two! You lead a low diamond, intending to finesse the queen. When the ◇K appears, your troubles are over. You will draw trumps and score the four diamond tricks that you need. Suppose instead that East holds ◇K-x-x. The ◇Q will win and you will draw trumps, ending in the dummy. You can then lead a diamond to the ten, picking up the suit for no losers and making the slam.

The situation would be exactly the same if the diamonds lay like this:

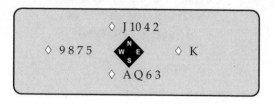

You would lead the ◊2 early in the play, to avoid losing a trick when East holds a singleton ◊K. If East played a low diamond and a finesse of the ◊Q succeeded. You would draw trumps, ending in the dummy and lead the ◊J to pick up a possible ◊K-x-x with East. (If East began with something like ◊K-9-7-5, you could not pick up the suit anyway.)

We will end the Tip with another situation that arises very frequently. Suppose you need to pick up this suit for no losers:

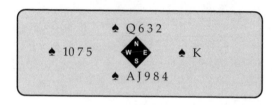

If you lead the ♠Q from dummy, you will soon regret it. East will cover with the singleton ♠K, won with the ♠A, and West's ♠10 will be promoted. A better idea is to lead a low card on the first round, following this Tip. If the singleton ♠K appears, all is well. Suppose instead that East plays low, you finesse the ♠J and West follows with the ♠10. You can return to dummy to pick up East's remaining ♠K-7. So, you will succeed against a singleton ♠K with East or a singleton ♠10 with West. You will win also, of course when East began with a doubleton ♠K.

(Leading the ♠Q on the first round does allow you to pick up ♠K-10-x with East, it is true, but only if you are willing to finesse the ♠10 on the second round after a Q/K/A cover on the first round. There is usually no reason to play in this way, since you would lose out when West holds a doubleton ♠10.)

Preserve your trumps when declarer is losing control

M any an interesting battle is fought when declarer's trump length is under attack and he is in danger of losing trump control. When you are defending in such a situation, you must be careful not to waste one of your trumps, handing control back to declarer. Take the East cards here:

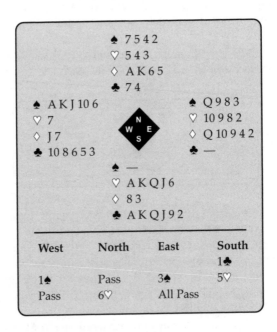

```
              ♠ 7 5 4 2
              ♡ 5 4 3
              ◇ A K 6 5
              ♣ 7 4
♠ A K J 10 6           ♠ Q 9 8 3
♡ 7              N      ♡ 10 9 8 2
◇ J 7         W   E    ◇ Q 10 9 4 2
♣ 10 8 6 5 3     S     ♣ —
              ♠ —
              ♡ A K Q J 6
              ◇ 8 3
              ♣ A K Q J 9 2
```

West	North	East	South
			1♣
1♠	Pass	3♠	5♡
Pass	6♡	All Pass	

South was fearful of opening 2♣ in case intervention came and he was unable to show his two suits. If you are not impressed by this argument, neither am I! Anyway, West led the ♠K and declarer ruffed with the ♡6.

Two rounds of trumps revealed the 4-1 trump break but all would still be well unless the club suit broke 5-0 too. Hoping to assist his cause if East was void in clubs, declarer crossed to the ◇A and led a club from dummy. How should you defend in the East seat?

Suppose you decide to score one of your trumps. You will ruff a loser and the slam will easily be made. Declarer can ruff your spade return, draw trumps and score all his clubs. You should not waste a precious trump in this way. Discard instead and declarer will win with the ♣A.

Declarer crosses to the ♦K and leads another club. You must discard again, retaining your trump length. Most players would have defended correctly up to this point. Now comes a sterner test. Declarer leads the ♣2 from his hand and ruffs with dummy's last trump, the ♡5. What now? If you overruff, you will reduce your trump length to one, compared with declarer's two. He will be able to ruff your spade return and draw trumps. Hard as it may seem, you should refuse to overruff.

Declarer is a doomed man. He is stuck in the dummy and cannot return to his hand to draw trumps. If he forces himself, by ruffing a spade or a diamond, you will have one trump more than him.

(Declarer should have abandoned trumps after one round. If he crosses to the ♦A at trick three to lead a club, you would have no defence.)

The last hand was not easy to defend, I concede, and neither is the next one! Still, take the West cards and see how you fare.

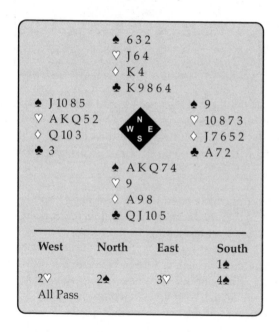

	♠ 6 3 2		
	♡ J 6 4		
	♦ K 4		
	♣ K 9 8 6 4		

♠ J 10 8 5   ♠ 9
♡ A K Q 5 2   ♡ 10 8 7 3
♦ Q 10 3   ♦ J 7 6 5 2
♣ 3   ♣ A 7 2

	♠ A K Q 7 4		
	♡ 9		
	♦ A 9 8		
	♣ Q J 10 5		

West	North	East	South
			1♠
2♡	2♠	3♡	4♠
All Pass			

You lead the ♡K and continue with the ♡A, declarer ruffing with the ♠4. He draws two rounds of trumps, East discarding a diamond on the second round. When declarer continues with the ♣Q, your partner wins with the ♣A and leads another heart, declarer ruffing with the ♠7. He and the dummy now hold one trump each, while you hold ♠J-10. How will you defend when declarer plays winning clubs, starting with the ♣J?

If you ruff the second, third or fourth round of clubs, the contract will be made. Declarer will be able to ruff your heart return with dummy's ♠6, cross to his hand with the ◇A and draw your last trump with the ♠Q. The remaining tricks will then be his. Instead you should preserve your trump length, discarding all three diamonds. These cards will then be left:

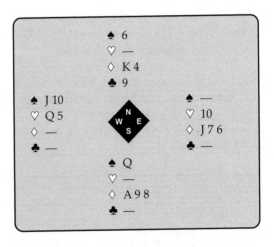

The contract is doomed. If declarer plays the ♣9, throwing a diamond, you will ruff with the ♠10 and return a heart. Declarer can ruff in the dummy but he will have no way to return to hand to draw your last trump. There will be the same outcome if declarer plays a diamond instead.

What was the important point on that last hand? You had to preserve your trump length until declarer could no longer get from the dummy to his hand, to draw your last trump.

(As on the first deal, declarer could have made his contract by playing more strongly. The winning line here was to draw just one round of trumps and then switch to clubs. He would then have an extra entry to his hand – a trump – at the key moment.)

Tip 41

Play the trump suit to keep the danger hand off lead

On some deals your play in the trump suit is dictated by the need to keep one of the defenders off lead. Would you have made this spade game?

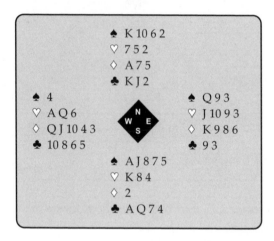

West leads the ◊Q, won in the dummy. How will you tackle the play?

With nine trumps between the hands, the 'normal' play is to cash the ace and king, hoping to drop the queen. It will lead to defeat on the lay-out shown. The queen will not fall and you will have to turn to the club suit in an effort to discard one of dummy's heart losers. All would be well if East followed to three clubs (you could discard one of dummy's hearts on the fourth round, not caring if East chose to ruff with his master trump). When East holds only two clubs, though, he can ruff the third club and defeat the contract by switching to the ♡J through your ♡K.

To prevent this unsavoury outcome, you must play trumps in such a way that East cannot gain the lead. You should play a trump to the king and then finesse the jack of trumps. When the cards lie as in the diagram, the finesse will win. You can draw the last trump and play on clubs, scoring an overtrick. Suppose the trump finesse had lost to a doubleton ♠Q, though. You would still make the contract. West could not attack diamonds successfully from his side of the table and you could discard

---

one of dummy's hearts on the fourth round of clubs.

Here is a more difficult deal on the same theme:

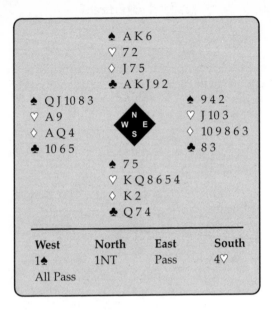

	♠ A K 6	
	♡ 7 2	
	◊ J 7 5	
	♣ A K J 9 2	
♠ Q J 10 8 3		♠ 9 4 2
♡ A 9		♡ J 10 3
◊ A Q 4		◊ 10 9 8 6 3
♣ 10 6 5		♣ 8 3
	♠ 7 5	
	♡ K Q 8 6 5 4	
	◊ K 2	
	♣ Q 7 4	

West	North	East	South
1♠	1NT	Pass	4♡
All Pass			

How will you play 4♡ when West leads the ♠Q, won in the dummy?

Suppose you play a trump to the king and ace, West continuing with another spade to dummy's king. You can draw a second round of trumps with the queen but you will now go down, whether you concede a third round of trumps or turn immediately to the club suit. East will gain the lead with his last trump and send a diamond through the king.

You cannot afford East to gain the lead and this should affect how you play the trumps. The best idea is to lead the ♡2 from dummy and cover East's ♡3 with the ♡4! West wins with the ♡9 but cannot play diamonds profitably from his side of the table. You win his spade continuation and play a second round of trumps to the king and ace. The best West can do now is to cash the ◊A. If he makes any other return, you will draw the last trump and discard both of your diamonds on dummy's club suit.

The 'normal play' with this heart holding is to lead a low card to the king, in the hope that East holds the ace. That could hardly be so here, because you are missing only 14 points and West opened the bidding.

We will end the Tip with a deal where you need to make two avoidance

Another 52 Great Bridge Tips

plays, one in the trump suit, to safeguard the contract.

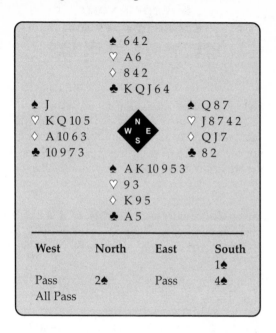

How will you play the spade game when West leads the ♡K?

Since you would not welcome a diamond lead from East, you must do what you can to keep him out of the lead. The first step in this direction is to duck the ♡K lead, just in case West could cross to the ♡J or ♡10 later in the play.

You win the next heart with dummy's ace and now have to consider your play in trumps. If you play the suit from the top, cashing the ♠A and ♠K, East will subsequently ruff the third round of clubs and put you one down you with a diamond switch. To prevent this, you should lead a spade to the ten. West wins with the bare ♠J but the contract is secure. The best West can do is to cash the ◇A. If instead he plays a club or a heart, you will win and draw trumps. You can then discard all your diamond losers on dummy's clubs.

Tip 42

Sharpen your bidding over an opponent's weak two

Bridge would be a more enjoyable game, perhaps, if the opponents were not allowed to pre-empt against you. How often do you pick up a great hand and hear some annoying pre-empt on your right? Well, life is not meant to be easy. In this Tip we will see some ways in which you can bid accurately when the opponents have opened with a weak-two bid.

Lebensohl opposite a take-out double of a weak two

Your main weapon, as in many situations, is the take-out double. In response to this, your partner should use the Lebensohl convention:

After a start such as:

West	North	East	South
	2♠	Dbl	Pass
?			

West will respond:

2NT	Lebensohl, 0-7 points. East usually rebids 3♣
3♣/3◇/3♡	Around 8-10 points, invitational
3♠	Game-forcing cue-bid

The bidding is basically the same over a weak 2♡, except that you can respond 2♠ on a weak hand with spades.

You use the 2NT response to sign off in an unbid suit:

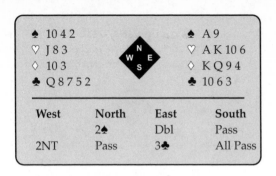

West	North	East	South
	2♠	Dbl	Pass
2NT	Pass	3♣	All Pass

Here West passes because his best suit is clubs.

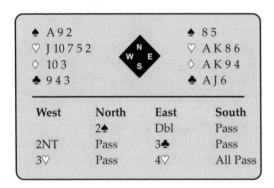

West	North	East	South
	2♠	Dbl	Pass
2NT	Pass	3♣	Pass
3♡	Pass	4♡	All Pass

West advances to 3♡, showing around 0-7 points and at least four hearts. Hoping that West does not hold a complete bust, East now guesses to bid 4♡.

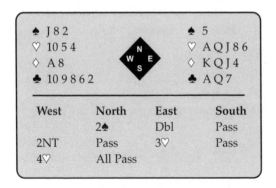

West	North	East	South
	2♠	Dbl	Pass
2NT	Pass	3♡	Pass
4♡	All Pass		

Here East has a strong hand for hearts and indicates this by bidding 3♡ instead of a passable 3♣. Since West has three-card heart support and an ace, he raises to game.

When responder shows a middle-range hand by bidding a suit at the three level, a change of suit continuation by the doubler is forcing:

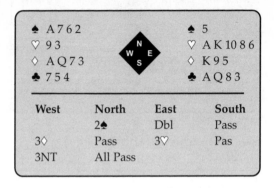

West	North	East	South
	2♠	Dbl	Pass
3◇	Pass	3♡	Pas
3NT	All Pass		

East decides to push on to game when he hears the 8-10 point 3◇ response. West cannot support the hearts but he is happy to bid 3NT. (Note that he could not respond with a natural 2NT initially because this would have been Lebensohl.)

Cue bid overcall to request a stopper

When you have an excellent minor suit, you can cue bid the opponent's suit. This asks partner to bid 3NT when he holds a stopper.

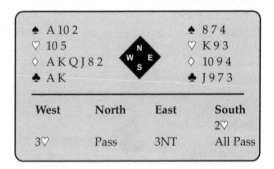

West	North	East	South
			2♡
3♡	Pass	3NT	All Pass

Here West has an obvious application of the cue-bid overcall. He would make the same bid with only ♠K-10-2 too, hoping for some assistance in partner's hand. Bidding is not a precise art (you may have noticed already!) and you must choose from the options available.

What should East do when he has no heart stopper? He can bid 3♠ with length in that suit, otherwise 4♣ so that West can sign off in his long suit. If East is very strong, with no stopper, he can make some higher bid.

Another 52 Great Bridge Tips

Leaping Michaels

What should it mean when an opponent opens 2♡ or 2♠ and you leap to 4♣? It is not particularly useful for this to be a natural bid, showing long clubs, because in that case you would be reluctant to bypass 3NT. It is better for the bid to show a two-suiter, at least 5-5 in the bid suit and the other major. The method is known as Leaping Michaels. (Yes, it's worth playing, if only for the splendid name!)

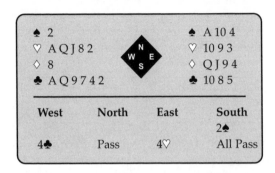

	♠ 2		♠ A 10 4
	♡ A Q J 8 2		♡ 10 9 3
	◊ 8		◊ Q J 9 4
	♣ A Q 9 7 4 2		♣ 10 8 5

West	North	East	South
			2♠
4♣	Pass	4♡	All Pass

West's 4♣ shows a two-suiter in hearts and clubs. With three-card heart support East chooses to play in the ten-trick game. Since he has a useful card in his hand (the ♠A), there is reasonable play for the contract. If East held a bust, of course, his side might well end up with a minus score. That is often the case when you enter the bidding after a pre-empt.

The Unusual 4NT

When you hold a similar two-suiter in the minors, you can overcall 4NT.

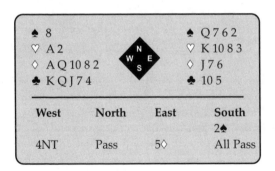

	♠ 8		♠ Q 7 6 2
	♡ A 2		♡ K 10 8 3
	◊ A Q 10 8 2		◊ J 7 6
	♣ K Q J 7 4		♣ 10 5

West	North	East	South
			2♠
4NT	Pass	5◊	All Pass

East has very little on this occasion and the game is not especially good. Still, it would be losing bridge to pass on powerful hands such as West's here. You have to take the plunge, expecting partner to hold something around 8 points on average.

Tip

43

**Avoid the finesse
that will cause
a blockage**

You take a finesse and, yes, it succeeds! When the suit becomes blocked as a result, the pleasure in the successful finesse will be short-lived. On the first deal, the potential blockage is in the trump suit. Would you have avoided the trap?

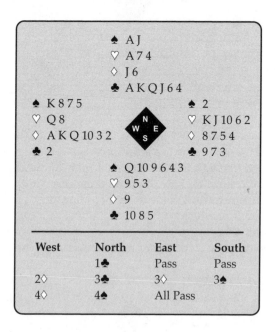

♠ A J
♡ A 7 4
♦ J 6
♣ A K Q J 6 4

♠ K 8 7 5
♡ Q 8
♦ A K Q 10 3 2
♣ 2

♠ 2
♡ K J 10 6 2
♦ 8 7 5 4
♣ 9 7 3

♠ Q 10 9 6 4 3
♡ 9 5 3
♦ 9
♣ 10 8 5

West	North	East	South
	1♣	Pass	Pass
2♦	3♣	3♦	3♠
4♦	4♠	All Pass	

West leads the ♦K, followed by the ♦A, which you ruff. There is a good chance that West holds the ♠K and you may be tempted to play a trump to jack next. See what happens if you do! East will show out when you continue with the ♠A. You can reach your hand with the ♣10 to lead the ♠Q but West will win with the ♠K and lock you in dummy with a heart. With no entry to your hand, you will not be able to prevent him from scoring a ruff with his ♠8. You will go two down.

Since you can afford to lose a trump trick, you should play a trump to the ace at trick two. You continue with the ♠J, overtaking in your hand with the ♠Q. West has to take his ♠K at some stage. When he does, you can win his return and enter your hand with the ♣10 to draw the remaining trumps. By giving up the trump finesse, you make an overtrick instead of going two down!

Here is another deal on the same theme, this time played in notrumps:

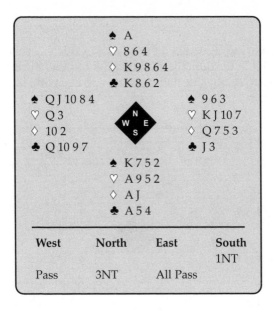

West	North	East	South
			1NT
Pass	3NT	All Pass	

West leads the ♠Q against 3NT. How will you play the contract?

Suppose you win with dummy's ♠A and finesse the ◊J. The finesse will win, yes, but the contract will then go down. With eight tricks on top, the best continuation is to cash the ◊A and duck a club. A 3-3 break in either minor would then see you home, but you will go down as the cards lie. If the finesse of the ◊J had lost to a doubleton ◊Q-x, you would have had no chance at all.

The best play in diamonds is to cross to the ◊A, to lead the ◊J back to dummy's ◊K and then to lead a third round of diamonds. You will make the four diamond tricks you need for the contract when diamonds break 3-3, also when the ◊Q or ◊10 is doubleton.

Tip 44

Use the surround play in defence

When your second and third ranked cards in a suit 'surround' a card in the dummy, it is often right to lead the higher of these cards through declarer. Not easy to visualize, it's true, so let's see an example.

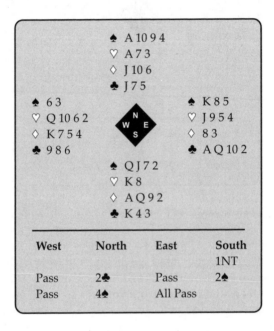

	♠ A 10 9 4	
	♡ A 7 3	
	◇ J 10 6	
	♣ J 7 5	
♠ 6 3		♠ K 8 5
♡ Q 10 6 2		♡ J 9 5 4
◇ K 7 5 4		◇ 8 3
♣ 9 8 6		♣ A Q 10 2
	♠ Q J 7 2	
	♡ K 8	
	◇ A Q 9 2	
	♣ K 4 3	

West	North	East	South
			1NT
Pass	2♣	Pass	2♠
Pass	4♠	All Pass	

It's not normally a good idea to bid Stayman when your hand is 4-3-3-3 shape (see Tip 2). Still, sitting East, the opponents' bidding style (or lack of it!) is no concern of yours. West leads the ♡2 and declarer wins your ♡J with the ♡K. At trick two he runs the ♠Q to your ♠K. What now?

It is very likely that you will need at least two club tricks to beat the game. Since your ♣Q-10 surround dummy's ♣J, you should switch to the ♣Q at trick three. Declarer covers with the ♣K, winning the trick, and draws trumps. When he subsequently runs the ◇J, luck turns against him. Your partner wins with the ◇K and switches back to clubs, allowing you to score two tricks in the suit.

As you see, it would be no good switching to the ♣2, or playing ace and another club. You needed to switch precisely to the queen of the suit.

Right, let's see another example. Take the East cards on this deal:

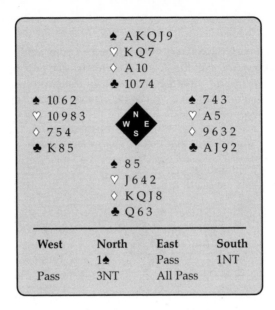

	♠ A K Q J 9		
	♡ K Q 7		
	◇ A 10		
	♣ 10 7 4		

West	North	East	South
	1♠	Pass	1NT
Pass	3NT	All Pass	

Your partner leads the ♡10 and you win dummy's ♡K with the ♡A. How will you continue the defence?

Let's count declarer's tricks. He has five spade tricks, two hearts (queen and jack) and the ◇A. That is eight certain tricks. If he holds the ♣K too, he will surely make the contract, so you must place that card with West. You need to score four club tricks in a hurry. How can it be done?

Suppose you lead the ♣2 next. Declarer may play low from his hand, forcing the ♣K from West. He will then have a stopper in the suit. Since your ♣J-9 surround dummy's ♣10, you should instead lead the ♣J at trick two. Declarer has no counter. If he plays low from his hand, you will continue with a low club to partner's ♣K and the suit will be yours. South will fare no better by covering with the ♣Q. Your partner will then win with the ♣K and return the ♣8 through dummy's remaining ♣10-7. Another triumph for the surround play!

Tip 45

Ruff the fourth round of a 4-3 side suit

Whit a four-card side suit in your hand with a three-card holding in the dummy, there are many occasions when it will pay you to attempt to ruff the fourth round of the suit. This is true even when dummy has relatively short trumps. Look at this deal:

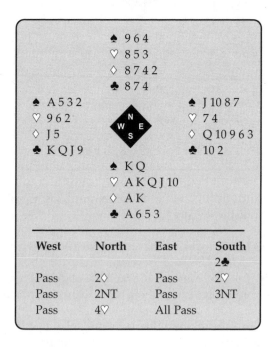

	♠ 9 6 4	
	♡ 8 5 3	
	◇ 8 7 4 2	
	♣ 8 7 4	

♠ A 5 3 2		♠ J 10 8 7
♡ 9 6 2		♡ 7 4
◇ J 5		◇ Q 10 9 6 3
♣ K Q J 9		♣ 10 2

	♠ K Q	
	♡ A K Q J 10	
	◇ A K	
	♣ A 6 5 3	

West	North	East	South
			2♣
Pass	2◇	Pass	2♡
Pass	2NT	Pass	3NT
Pass	4♡	All Pass	

3NT would have been easier, yes, but how will you play the heart game when West leads the ♣K?

If you win with the ♣A and draw trumps, you will need a 3-3 club break. This is a poor chance, particularly when West has indicated a sequence in clubs and is therefore likely to hold at least four cards in the suit.

A better idea is to play for a club ruff in dummy. Win the club lead and return a club. If West continues clubs, ruff the fourth round with dummy's ♡8. Since East does not hold the ♡9, he will not be able to overruff. You can then draw trumps and force out the ♠A, claiming the contract.

Suppose that West switches to a trump when he wins the second club. You win and give up another club trick. East shows out on the third round of clubs and West returns another trump. All is still well. When you lead your last club and ruff with the ♡8, East cannot overruff because West has the missing ♡9. You would make the contract also if East had started with ♡7-x-x. Once again, he would not be able to overruff.

When you hold the three top honours in the 4-3 suit, it will often be right to test the lie of the defenders' cards in the suit before drawing all the trumps. Many players would go down on this simple-looking deal:

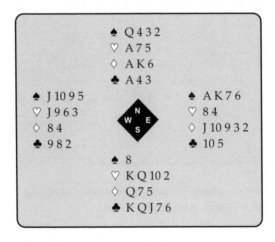

```
                    ♠ Q 4 3 2
                    ♡ A 7 5
                    ◇ A K 6
                    ♣ A 4 3
♠ J 10 9 5                         ♠ A K 7 6
♡ J 9 6 3          N               ♡ 8 4
◇ 8 4          W       E           ◇ J 10 9 3 2
♣ 9 8 2            S               ♣ 10 5
                    ♠ 8
                    ♡ K Q 10 2
                    ◇ Q 7 5
                    ♣ K Q J 7 6
```

West leads the ♠J against 6♣. You play low in the dummy (since there is some chance of ruffing out ♠A-K-x with East) and West continues with the ♠10, which you ruff. What now?

If you draw trumps, hoping that the heart suit will provide four tricks, you will be disappointed. A better idea is to play the ♣A-K and to test the hearts. You play the ♡K, ♡A and then lead dummy's ♡7. East shows out but has no trump left. You win with the ♡Q and ruff your fourth heart. You can then cross to the ◇Q and draw the last trump.

Playing in this way costs you absolutely nothing. If one of the hearts is ruffed, you would also have gone down by drawing trumps straight away. What you gain is the chance to make the contract when the player who is short in hearts also holds a doubleton (or singleton) trump.

When your side suit is something like A-x-x-x opposite K-x-x, you may need to duck an early round. Why is that? Because you intend to draw precisely two rounds of trumps before seeking the ruff. By ducking an early round of the side suit, you will maintain control of the trump situation. That's what happens on this deal:

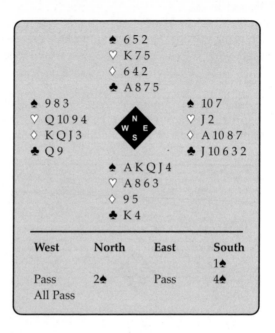

♠ 6 5 2
♡ K 7 5
◇ 6 4 2
♣ A 8 7 5

♠ 9 8 3   ♠ 10 7
♡ Q 10 9 4   ♡ J 2
◇ K Q J 3   ◇ A 10 8 7
♣ Q 9   ♣ J 10 6 3 2

♠ A K Q J 4
♡ A 8 6 3
◇ 9 5
♣ K 4

West	North	East	South
			1♠
Pass	2♠	Pass	4♠
All Pass			

The defenders play three rounds of diamonds and you ruff the third round with the ♠4. How will you continue?

You can escape for one heart loser when the suit breaks 3-3 or you can ruff the fourth round in the dummy. Since dummy's highest trump is the ♠6, you can score a ruff only when the defender with a doubleton heart began with only two trumps. Even then, you will need to play carefully.

Suppose you draw two rounds of trumps and then play ace, king and another heart. That's no good. When West wins the third round of hearts, he will be able to lead a third round of trumps, removing dummy's last trump. And if East had held the last trump, he would have been able to overruff the dummy anyway.

How should you play the contract? You should draw one round of trumps with the ♠A and duck the first round of hearts. (If instead you duck the second round, East will score a heart ruff). You win the return, play the ♠K and the king and ace of hearts. If the hearts break 3-3, you will draw the last trump. When the cards lie as in the diagram, East will show out on the third heart but will have no trumps left. You can ruff your fourth heart in the dummy.

We will end the Tip with a deal where you cannot stop a defender from scoring a ruff, but you can make sure that he does not ruff an honour.

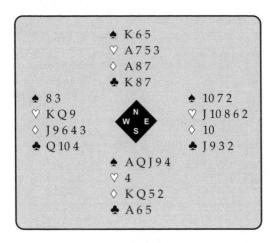

You bid to 6♠ and West leads a trump. How will you play the slam?

You win the trump lead in the South hand and draw a second round of trumps, leaving the ♠K in dummy. The idea now is to play three rounds of diamonds. If the suit breaks 3-3 you will make the contract easily. If the defender who is short in diamonds does not hold the last trump, you will be able to ruff your fourth diamond in the dummy.

You can also make the slam when East is short in diamonds and does hold the last trump. You cross to the ◇A and lead a diamond towards your hand. East has no diamonds left. If he ruffs a diamond spot-card, however, you will be able to throw one of dummy's clubs on the fourth round of diamonds and score a club ruff in dummy as your twelfth trick.

Let's suppose that East discards a club. You win with the ◇K, cross to dummy with the ♣K and lead a third round of diamonds towards your hand. Once again, East cannot beat you by ruffing. If he discards, you will win with the ◇Q and ruff the fourth round of diamonds with dummy's ♠K. Slam bid, slam made!

Tip

46

Do not bid a minor unless you would welcome support

When your partner opens 1NT, whether weak or strong, you will have a pretty good idea of the playing strength of the two hands. As responder, you should not introduce a minor suit, on the way to game, unless there is a reasonable chance of making at least eleven tricks with that suit as trumps. When your hand is much more likely to produce nine tricks in 3NT, do not even mention the minor suit.

Suppose you play that a direct response of 3♣ or 3◊ is natural and forcing to game, which of these hands would be worth such a bid, facing a 12-14 point 1NT?

(1)	(2)	(3)
♠ J 5	♠ K 9 5	♠ A K 4
♡ K 4	♡ 7	♡ 6
◊ J 9 2	◊ A K 10 8 6 4	◊ Q 8 3
♣ A Q 10 7 5 2	♣ 10 8 4	♣ A J 10 8 7 2

Hand (1) is unlikely to produce eleven tricks in clubs, with only a weak 1NT opposite. You should raise 1NT to 3NT. If instead you responded 3♣, a good partner would raise you when he held good club support and that would carry you past 3NT. He would (or should) say to himself: 'There would be no point introducing the clubs unless he wanted me to show support'. Quite right!

Hand (2) is similar. You may be worried about the singleton heart, playing in 3NT. Indeed, the hearts may be under protected. If you bid all the way to 5◊, however, you are likely to find that you are short of the values to make eleven tricks. (This is only one trick short of a slam, remember.) So, again the best response is to raise to 3NT.

Only on hand (3) can you expect to make eleven tricks if there is a good club fit. On that hand it would be reasonable to respond 3♣.

The same concept applies when you hold a five-card major and a four-card minor. Suppose, this time, that partner has opened a strong 1NT of 15-17 points and you hold one of these hands:

	(4)		(5)		(6)
♠	10 3	♠	K Q 10 8 2	♠	4
♡	A J 8 7 2	♡	4	♡	A K 10 8 2
◇	8 5	◇	9 7 2	◇	A Q 10 4
♣	K Q 7 2	♣	K J 9 4	♣	J 9 8

You respond 2◇ – a transfer bid, showing five hearts – on hand (4) and partner duly rebids 2♡. What next? A rebid of 3♣ would be natural and forcing to game but it is the wrong continuation. With only 10 points, you want partner to choose between 4♡ and 3NT, since you cannot expect eleven tricks with clubs as trumps. So, you should rebid 3NT instead.

(By the way, some players treat 3♣ as 'forcing to 3♡'. This is an unsound method, because when the opener is minimum and has only two hearts, you will have to play in 3♡, which is unlikely to be the best contract. When you have only game-try values in response, you should rebid 2NT rather than 3♣. You can then stop in 2NT, the best contract available, when the opener holds two hearts and a minimum.)

On hand (5) you may be nervous of 3NT because of the singleton heart. Still, you should follow a 2♡ transfer bid with 3NT. It is not right to introduce the clubs because you cannot expect to make eleven tricks with clubs as trumps and would not therefore welcome a raise. A good partner will raise 3♣ to 4♣ when he has club support. Again he would not expect you to bid the suit unless there were some point in doing so.

Only on hand (6) should you follow your transfer response (2◇) with a bid that shows your second suit (3◇). That's because you have a stronger hand and can expect to make eleven, or even twelve, tricks in diamonds if partner has a good fit there.

Finally, the same Tip can be applied to Stayman sequences. Suppose your partner opens a 12-14 point 1NT and you hold one of these hands:

(7)	(8)	(9)
♠ 9 4	♠ K Q 8 2	♠ A Q 10 6
♡ A Q 8 7	♡ 4	♡ 7 4
◇ J 5	◇ A J 9 7 2	◇ A 2
♣ K Q 7 5 2	♣ Q 9 5	♣ A K 10 8 3

On hand (7) you respond with a Stayman 2♣, in case there is a 4-4 heart fit. If partner responds 2♠ or 2◇, you have the option of bidding 3♣, which would be natural and forcing to game. It is not the right continuation on this hand, however. Facing a weak 1NT you cannot expect there to be eleven tricks in clubs. (Yes, there might be, but it is not very likely.) So you should bid 3NT at your second turn.

It's the same on (8). After 1NT – 2♣ – 2◇/2♡, you should rebid 3NT. You are not strong enough to suggest a diamond game by rebidding 3◇. Remember that the sequence 1NT – 2♣ – 2♡ – 3NT promises four spades. You would not have bid Stayman otherwise. The opener will correct to 4♠ when he holds four spades as well as four hearts.

Hand (9) is more like it! After 1NT – 2♣ – 2◇/2♡, you will continue with 3♣, natural and forcing to game. You want partner to raise you when he has club support. Indeed, there is a fair chance of a slam in the suit when partner has a fit. By rebidding 3♣, you invite partner to raise the clubs. A good partner will not woodenly rebid 3NT just because he has the red suits well stopped. He will know that you are looking for club support when you bother to show the suit opposite a 1NT opening.

Discard a
blocking honour

'It was awkward, because the diamonds were blocked!' How often have you heard players saying something like that? One of the ways in which you can counter a blockage is to discard the blocking card. Here is a straightforward example:

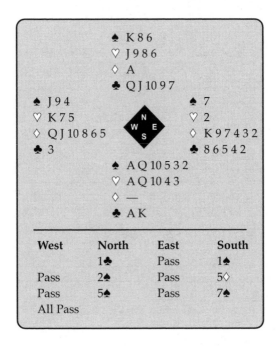

	♠ K 8 6		
	♡ J 9 8 6		
	◇ A		
	♣ Q J 10 9 7		

♠ J 9 4
♡ K 7 5
◇ Q J 10 8 6 5
♣ 3

♠ 7
♡ 2
◇ K 9 7 4 3 2
♣ 8 6 5 4 2

♠ A Q 10 5 3 2
♡ A Q 10 4 3
◇ —
♣ A K

West	North	East	South
	1♣	Pass	1♠
Pass	2♠	Pass	5◇
Pass	5♠	Pass	7♠
All Pass			

South's 5◇ was Exclusion Blackwood, asking for key cards with the ◇A not included. North's response showed one key card, which had to be the ♣K, and South then gambled on a grand slam. If North did not hold the ♡K, he might hold a good enough club suit to throw all the heart losers. Failing that, declarer could fall back on a heart finesse. Anyway, how would you play the grand slam when West leads the ◇Q?

You can see thirteen tricks (six spades, five clubs and two red aces) but… the club suit is blocked. To protect yourself against a 5-1 club break, you should discard the ♣A or ♣K on the first trick. You draw two rounds of trumps with the ace and queen, East showing out on the second round.

You then cash your remaining club honour, everyone following. Finally, you cross to dummy with the ♠K and run the remaining club tricks, discarding four hearts from your hand. As you see, you would go down if you discarded a heart at trick one. You would then have to cash the ♣A-K before crossing to dummy with the ♠K. West would ruff the second club.

Would you have spotted the need for a similar play on the next deal?

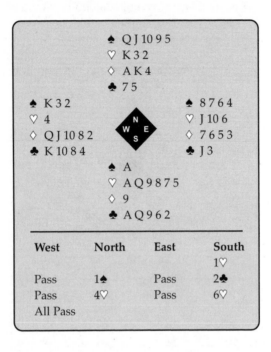

West	North	East	South
			1♡
Pass	1♠	Pass	2♣
Pass	4♡	Pass	6♡
All Pass			

How will you play the slam when West leads the ◊Q, won with the ◊A?

Only one action at trick two will be good enough. You must lead the ◊K and discard the blocking ♠A. You then run the ♠Q, throwing a club loser from your hand. If West chooses to duck a round or two of spades, you continue to run spades to him, discarding further clubs. When you regain the lead, you will draw trumps in three rounds, ending in the dummy. You can then enjoy the rest of the spade suit.

Tip 48

Do not give partner a chance to go wrong

Wfhen you can see what the winning defence will be, you must try to make life easy for your partner. Take the West cards here:

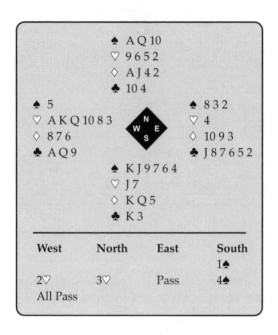

```
                    ♠ A Q 10
                    ♡ 9 6 5 2
                    ◇ A J 4 2
                    ♣ 10 4
   ♠ 5                              ♠ 8 3 2
   ♡ A K Q 10 8 3       N           ♡ 4
   ◇ 8 7 6            W   E          ◇ 10 9 3
   ♣ A Q 9              S            ♣ J 8 7 6 5 2
                    ♠ K J 9 7 6 4
                    ♡ J 7
                    ◇ K Q 5
                    ♣ K 3
```

West	North	East	South
			1♠
2♡	3♡	Pass	4♠
All Pass			

Sitting West, you lead the ♡K against the spade game. East follows with the ♡4 and South plays the ♡J. How will you continue the defence?

How do the hearts lie? South has dropped the ♡J, but East would not have played the ♡4 from ♡7-4. So, South still holds the ♡7 and another heart will stand up. Suppose you play the ♡A next. Partner may well discard and there will be no way to beat the contract. When declarer gains the lead, he will draw trumps and discard one of his club losers.

"Why didn't you ruff my ♡A and switch to a club, partner?" you exclaim. "We take the first four tricks!"

Yes, but you are the one who can see that a club lead from East will give

---

you two tricks in the suit. It is therefore your duty to lead the ♡3 at trick two, forcing East to ruff. His club switch will then beat the game.

The situation illustrated by the next deal arises time and time again.

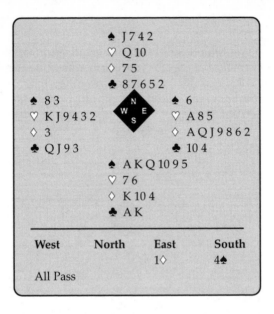

```
                    ♠ J 7 4 2
                    ♡ Q 10
                    ◇ 7 5
                    ♣ 8 7 6 5 2
    ♠ 8 3           ┌─────┐        ♠ 6
    ♡ K J 9 4 3 2   │  N  │        ♡ A 8 5
    ◇ 3             │W ◆ E│        ◇ A Q J 9 8 6 2
    ♣ Q J 9 3       │  S  │        ♣ 10 4
                    └─────┘
                    ♠ A K Q 10 9 5
                    ♡ 7 6
                    ◇ K 10 4
                    ♣ A K
```

West	North	East	South
		1◇	4♠
All Pass			

You are sitting East and your partner leads the ◇3 to your ◇A. What card will you play next?

At the table East returned the ◇Q, his highest diamond to request a heart return (in other words, it was a suit preference signal). South covered with the ◇K and West ruffed. Two tricks for the defence, then, but what should West play next? Rightly or wrongly, he viewed partner's ◇Q as the natural card to lead from ◇Q-J through declarer's ◇K, not necessarily a suit preference signal. Reluctant to lead from the ♡K with the ♡Q visible in the dummy, West switched to the ♣Q.

Declarer won in his hand and drew one round of trumps with the ace. He then cashed his other top club and crossed to dummy with the ten of trumps to the jack. A club ruff was followed by a trump to the seven and another club ruff. Declarer reached the established long card in clubs with a diamond ruff and discarded one of his heart losers.

East complained loudly at his partner's failure to switch to a heart. He was largely to blame himself, however. Before delivering the diamond ruff, he should play the ♡A. It is then easy for West to cash the ♡K.

Tip
49

Rise with dummy's ace to restrict the danger

When you are playing in no-trumps, you must think carefully before allowing your right-hand opponent to win the first trick. If he might be able to inflict some damage with his return, it may be better to win the opening lead with dummy's ace. Test yourself on this deal:

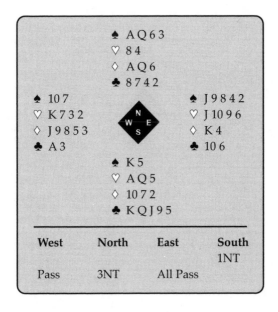

```
                    ♠ A Q 6 3
                    ♡ 8 4
                    ◊ A Q 6
                    ♣ 8 7 4 2
    ♠ 10 7                         ♠ J 9 8 4 2
    ♡ K 7 3 2          N           ♡ J 10 9 6
    ◊ J 9 8 5 3    W       E       ◊ K 4
    ♣ A 3              S           ♣ 10 6
                    ♠ K 5
                    ♡ A Q 5
                    ◊ 10 7 2
                    ♣ K Q J 9 5
```

West	North	East	South
			1NT
Pass	3NT	All Pass	

How will you play 3NT when West leads the ◊5?

Suppose you are tempted to play the ◊Q from dummy. You will soon regret it. East will win with the ◊K and return a diamond, the defenders clearing the suit. When you subsequently play on clubs, West will win with the ace and cash his remaining diamonds to put you one down.

The safest line is to rise with the ◊A at trick one and then play clubs. If East holds the ♣A, you will be 100% secure. Even if West produces the ♣A, it is almost impossible for the defenders to claim four diamond tricks at that point. (When the cards lie as in the diagram, East will win dummy's ◊Q with the ◊K on the second round but the suit will be

---

blocked. You would go down only when the opening lead was from ◊5-4 or ◊5-3.)

Perhaps you would have played the ◊6 on the first trick. East would win with the ◊K and switch to the ♡J. As the cards lie, you could survive by applying this Tip at trick two! You would rise with the ♡A and play clubs. Since by good fortune West holds the ♣A, the hearts would be preserved from attack from his side of the table. You would go down, however, if East held the ♣A and could persist with hearts through your ♡Q. So, much the best idea is to win the first trick with dummy's ◊A.

Let's see another deal on this theme:

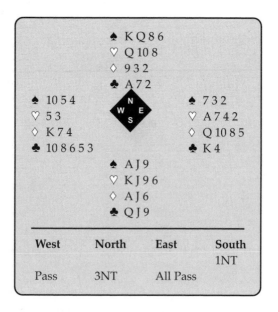

	♠ K Q 8 6		
	♡ Q 10 8		
	◊ 9 3 2		
	♣ A 7 2		

♠ 10 5 4		♠ 7 3 2
♡ 5 3		♡ A 7 4 2
◊ K 7 4		◊ Q 10 8 5
♣ 10 8 6 5 3		♣ K 4

	♠ A J 9		
	♡ K J 9 6		
	◊ A J 6		
	♣ Q J 9		

West	North	East	South
			1NT
Pass	3NT	All Pass	

How will you play 3NT when West leads the ♣5?

Playing on auto-pilot, you might well play low from dummy. Not the best! East will win with the ♣K and may switch to the ◊10 (a surround-play, as described in Tip 44). However you play to the second trick, you will lose three diamonds, one club and one heart, going one down.

Playing on auto-pilot is always a second-best idea compared with making a plan! Here you have six tricks on top. Since you can easily establish three more tricks in hearts, you should rise with the ♣A at trick one and play on hearts. The defenders will then have no chance to beat you.

Tip 50

Overcall on a strong four-card suit

The general guidelines for making an overcall are that you should hold a five-card suit at the one-level and a six-card suit at the two-level. That's sound enough advice but there are occasions where you should overcall with a four-card suit at the one-level. Your hand should fit into this category:

- you have enough points for an opening bid
- your four-card suit is strong
- you have length in the opponent's suit

The fact that you are long in the suit that has been opened will mean that your shape is unsuitable for a take-out double. Suppose the player in front of you has opened 1♣ and you hold one of these hands:

	(1)	(2)	(3)
♠	A K Q 7	K 9 3	A 8 7 2
♡	8	A K J 7	9
◇	J 8 7 2	4	K Q J 9
♣	A 10 8 2	K J 7 5 4	A 8 5 3

Don't think twice about overcalling 1♠ on (1). It is the right action! There are so many advantages to the bid. You prevent a 1♡ response from your left-hand opponent (LHO). You also get into the bidding and allow partner to compete in spades when he has some support for you. You suggest a good opening lead for your partner, should your LHO play the contract. Finally, on some deals (not here) your opponents will expect you to hold a five-card suit and may be frightened from playing in a cold 3NT.

On (2) you want to enter the auction but your hand is unsuitable for a take-out double, since partner may well respond in diamonds and you would have no sound continuation. Overcall 1♡. You are one heart short, yes, but your 15 points will make up for that. Hand (3) is again unsuitable for a take-out double of 1♣ because of the heart shortage. Overcall 1◇ instead, bidding the suit that has some substance.

Note that all the above hands follow the three guidelines that were given: a hand worth an opening bid, a strong four-card suit and length in the opponent's suit. Let's see some hands that do not follow all the guidelines and are therefore unsuitable for a one-level overcall. Suppose, again, that your RHO has opened 1♣ and you hold one of these hands:

(4)	(5)	(6)
♠ A J 6 3	♠ A 8 5	♠ K Q J 9
♡ 7	♡ A Q J 10	♡ 8 3
◇ A J 7 2	◇ 10 9 6 4	◇ K 10 5
♣ K 10 8 2	♣ K 8	♣ 10 7 4 3

On hand (4) neither your spades nor your diamonds are strong enough for a one-level overcall on a four-card suit. You cannot risk a take-out double with only one heart, so you should pass. You could overcall 1♡ on hand (5), to suggest a good lead, but it is much better to start with a take-out double. Partner might hold only two hearts and some length in either spades or diamonds. Hand (6) has a strong enough spade suit but only 9 high-card points. That is too weak for a four-card overcall and you should pass.

Do overcalls on a four-card suit cause any problem when your partner has a good hand in response? Not really. If he has a strong hand with only three-card support, he will begin with a cue-bid in the opener's suit. You can then bid no-trumps, to suggest that you hold only four cards in your suit, a good hand, and a stopper in the suit opened. If instead partner holds at least four-card support and leaps pre-emptively to the three- or four-level, your extra high-card points will make up for the lack of a fifth trump.

You've never overcalled on a four-card suit in your life before? You only live once, my friend. Give the method a try!

Tip 51

Swap one ruff for another

When you are in danger of being overruffed in one suit, it may be a good idea to discard instead and take the ruff later in a safer suit. Let's see an example of this technique:

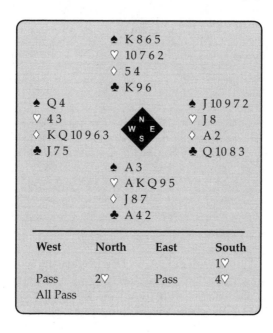

	♠ K 8 6 5	
	♡ 10 7 6 2	
	◊ 5 4	
	♣ K 9 6	
♠ Q 4		♠ J 10 9 7 2
♡ 4 3		♡ J 8
◊ K Q 10 9 6 3		◊ A 2
♣ J 7 5		♣ Q 10 8 3
	♠ A 3	
	♡ A K Q 9 5	
	◊ J 8 7	
	♣ A 4 2	

West	North	East	South
			1♡
Pass	2♡	Pass	4♡
All Pass			

West leads the ◊K and East overtakes with the ◊A. Back comes the ◊2 to your ◊J and West's ◊Q. How will you play the contract when West continues with the ◊10?

The defenders' antics make it likely that diamonds are 6-2. Suppose you ruff the third round of diamonds with dummy's ♡10 and East overruffs with the ♡J. You will have no way to avoid the subsequent loss of a club trick and will go one down.

Whether or not it is likely that diamonds are 6-2, there is no need to take such a risk. You should discard one of dummy's clubs on the third round of diamonds. A further round of diamonds would pose no problem. You will win West's switch to any other suit, draw trumps and eventually ruff a club loser in dummy. By swapping a dangerous diamond ruff for a safe club ruff, you make the contract.

Here is another deal on the same theme:

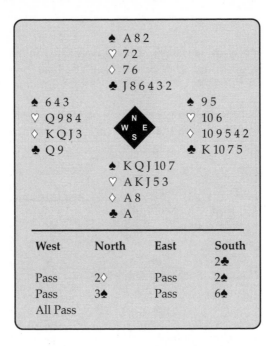

	♠ A 8 2	
	♡ 7 2	
	◇ 7 6	
	♣ J 8 6 4 3 2	

♠ 6 4 3			♠ 9 5
♡ Q 9 8 4			♡ 10 6
◇ K Q J 3			◇ 10 9 5 4 2
♣ Q 9			♣ K 10 7 5

	♠ K Q J 10 7	
	♡ A K J 5 3	
	◇ A 8	
	♣ A	

West	North	East	South
			2♣
Pass	2◇	Pass	2♠
Pass	3♣	Pass	6♠
All Pass			

West led the ◇K, won with the ◇A, and the original declarer set about the heart suit immediately. He cashed the ace and king successfully and led a third round, the ♡9 appearing from West. Declarer could now see two chances of making the slam. 'Ruff with the eight, please,' he said.

If hearts had been 3-3 or West had held the ♠9, the slam would have been made. Unfortunately, the cards were not placed so helpfully. East overruffed with the ♠9 and returned a diamond to put the slam one down. 'Not my lucky day,' muttered declarer.

It could have been declarer's lucky day, had he played the hand differently. He should have ruffed the third round of hearts with the ♠A. If the heart suit turned out to be 3-3, he could then simply draw trumps. With the cards lying as they were, he would return to his hand with the ♣A and lead a fourth round of hearts, discarding dummy's last diamond. Nothing could then prevent him from ruffing a diamond for his twelfth trick. In effect, he would have swapped a dangerous heart ruff for a safe diamond ruff.

In the final example, you have to swap a dangerous overruff with a safe ruff! Take a look at this:

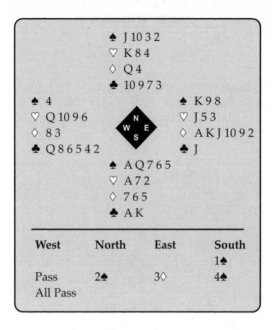

West leads the ♢8 and East wins the first two tricks with the ♢J and the ♢K. He continues with the ♢9 at trick three and West ruffs with the ♠4. How will you play the contract?

East's ♢9 was a winner. Why do you think that West has ruffed it? It is an attempted uppercut. He hopes that if you overruff with dummy's jack or ten, this will promote a trump trick for East. It could just happen, too, if the ♠4 is a singleton and East holds ♠K-9-8. In that case you would lose a trump trick and an eventual heart trick, going one down.

Since the overruff is dangerous and might promote a trump trick for East, you should discard a heart from dummy instead of overruffing. Let's say that West switches to a club. You win with the ♣A, cross to the ♡K and lead the ♠J. You run this card and pick up East's trumps in two more rounds. You can then take an oh-so-safe heart ruff.

Tip 52   Be wary of splitting your honours

Suppose you are defending in the second seat and have touching honours in the suit that declarer has just led. Perhaps you are tempted to play one of those honours. It will often cost you a trick! You are West here:

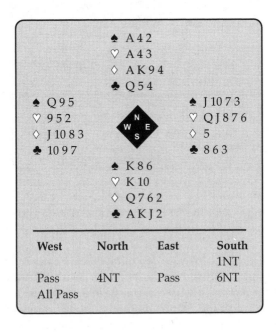

	♠ A 4 2	
	♡ A 4 3	
	◇ A K 9 4	
	♣ Q 5 4	
♠ Q 9 5		♠ J 10 7 3
♡ 9 5 2		♡ Q J 8 7 6
◇ J 10 8 3		◇ 5
♣ 10 9 7		♣ 8 6 3
	♠ K 8 6	
	♡ K 10	
	◇ Q 7 6 2	
	♣ A K J 2	

West	North	East	South
			1NT
Pass	4NT	Pass	6NT
All Pass			

Following a Tip from the original book, *52 Great Bridge Tips*, you seek a safe lead against 6NT, selecting the ♣10. Declarer wins with the ♣A and leads the ◇2 from his hand. How will you defend?

It would be foolish to split your diamond honours. Declarer would win with the ◇A and return to the ◇Q, East showing out. He would then finesse dummy's ◇9, scoring the four diamond tricks he needs.

Play low on the first diamond and there is no reason to expect declarer to finesse the ◇9. Also, your partner might hold a singleton ◇Q. Split your honours in that case and declarer might make a slam that was destined to fail.

It is the same when declarer leads a low card towards the closed hand. In many cases there is nothing to be gained in splitting your honours.

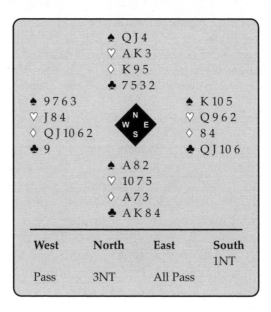

West	North	East	South
			1NT
Pass	3NT	All Pass	

You are sitting East and partner leads the ◊Q. Declarer wins with dummy's ◊K and leads the ♣2 towards his hand. How will you defend?

It may seem natural to insert the ♣Q but it will give declarer the contract. He will win with the ♣A and your partner will contribute the ♣9. A low club to dummy's seven will force another of your honours, West showing out. You can clear the diamonds but declarer will subsequently run the ♠Q and finesse the ♣8 to bring his total to nine.

Play low on the first club and declarer will go down. Perhaps you are worried that declarer has ♣A-K-9 and playing low will allow him to finesse the ♣9. If that is his holding, he can make three club tricks however you defend. If you split your honours on the first round he will win, return to dummy and lead another club. You will have to split your remaining honours and West's ♣8 will fall under South's honour. He can then lead the ♣9 to set up dummy's ♣7.

There are various situations where splitting honours can help declarer to guess a suit correctly. Look at this diamond situation:

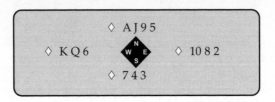

◇ A J 9 5

◇ K Q 6   **N W E S**   ◇ 10 8 2

◇ 7 4 3

Play low when the ◇3 is led and declarer will call for the ◇9, losing to East's ◇10. If instead you play the ◇K or ◇Q, he may play you for the ◇K-Q, winning with the ace and leading to the jack subsequently.

We will end the Tip with a deal where the right defence is surprising:

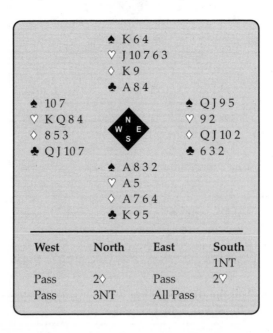

West	North	East	South
			1NT
Pass	2◇	Pass	2♡
Pass	3NT	All Pass	

Sitting West, you lead the ♣Q against 3NT. Declarer wins with the ♣K and plays the ♡A, followed by the ♡5. How will you defend?

Suppose you win with the ♡Q and clear the clubs. Declarer will lead the ♡J to your ♡K and soon have nine tricks. Try playing low smoothly on the second heart! A good declarer will duck in the dummy, gaining when East holds ♡K-x or ♡Q-x. (His play makes no difference when hearts are 3-3.) East will win with the bare ♡9 and declarer will go one down!